BRAIN-BOOSTING
MATH

Grades 5–6

Todd

By Jillayne Prince Wallaker

Cover Design by
Matthew Van Zomeren

Illustrations by
Marty Bucella

Carson-Dellosa Publishing Company, Inc.
Greensboro, North Carolina

Dedication
To my family with love.
Also to LCII—thank you for making
it through one last manuscript.

Credits

Author: Jillayne Prince Wallaker
Artist: Marty Bucella
Cover Art Direction: Annette Hollister-Papp
Cover Design: Matthew Van Zomeren
Editors: Kelly Morris Huxmann, Elizabeth Flikkema
Graphic Design and Layout: Mark Conrad, River Road Graphics

Printed in the USA • All rights reserved

ISBN: 0-88724-934-5

Table of Contents

Determining Order

Follow the directions for each problem.

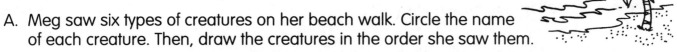

A. Meg saw six types of creatures on her beach walk. Circle the name of each creature. Then, draw the creatures in the order she saw them.

Meg saw the octopus before the clams. The seagulls were soaring overhead when she arrived at the beach. Meg had the starfish in her hand when she saw the fish; that was before the clams or octopus. A dolphin surfaced just as she was leaving.

B. Ian's family went to the museum. Put the locations of their visit in order. Then, name one thing they may have seen in each area that would be exclusive to the area.

The mammals section was first. The bird area was not visited last. The aquatic area was seen before the insect area but after the reptile room. The reptile room was not the second stop. They had lunch after visiting the third section.

C. Jade went on a hike. Write or draw the things she saw in the order she saw them.

Jade picked up some pinecones just before arriving at the waterfall. She spotted the coyote second. She saw the wild blueberries before the waterfall. Jade had a pinecone in her pocket when she climbed the boulder, but it fell from her pocket as she climbed the steps to the observation platform where she saw an eagle. From there, she went home.

Write your own on the back of this page.

I. Choose six objects. Write them in order.

2. Write the name of each object on a separate piece of paper. Then, write two clues. Give hints in the clues about the order of the objects. Only tell exactly where one object is.

3. Place as many of the objects in order as you can using the two clues. Then, add one clue at a time until all the objects are in the correct order. Use ordinal numbers and words like "before," "after," and "next to."

4. Check for accuracy. Make corrections. Rewrite your clues neatly on a 3" x 5" card. Put the clues card and objects (pictures or names) in a bag for someone else to put in order.

Math Journal

mathematical reasoning

Follow the directions to complete the sample math-journal page below.
Then, complete the journal entries on page 7.

1. The question or statement that needs proving is called the **premise**.
   The premise is at the top of the journal page. Underline the premise with red.

2. One fraction is given. Write two additional fractions. Draw an arrow to each denominator
   and write the word "denominator."

3. The space below the premise is the **illustration** area.
   Trace around this area with blue.

4. Below the illustration is the **explanation** area. Look at the fractions you wrote.
   What is the bottom number called? _____

5. Read the explanation. Fill in the blanks. The explanation always refers to the illustration.
   Circle the sentence that refers to the drawing with yellow.

Name: _____   Date: _____

What is a denominator?

denominator ⟍
              $\dfrac{4}{5}$

The _____ is the bottom number of a _____.

It tells the total number of equal _____. In the fractions above, the

_____ , _____ , and _____ are all _____.

Math Journal (continued)

Name: _____ Date: _____

Prove that $\frac{1}{3}$ and $\frac{2}{6}$ are equivalent fractions.

Draw a fraction bar divided into thirds. Shade one space.
Draw an arrow to the shaded space and write " $\frac{1}{3}$." Draw a second fraction bar the same size
divided into sixths. Shade two spaces. Draw an arrow to the shaded spaces and write " $\frac{2}{6}$."

_____ fractions are fractions that take up an equal amount of space.

In the diagram above, _____ and _____ use up the same

amount of space so they are _____ _____ .

Name: _____ Date: _____

What is a product?

Write two multiplication sentences here. Draw an arrow to each answer and write "product."

The _____ is the answer to a multiplication problem.

In the problems above, _____ and _____ are products.

Have your students keep math journals following the template presented on pages 6 and 7. Use the premises listed below or generate your own.

To make the journal: Cut a sheet of white paper in half. Staple together to make a four-page booklet. Have students write one premise at the top of each page or cut and paste some of the premises below. Use the checklist on page 9 as a guide.

--✂

What is an inverse operation?

How is a scalene triangle different from a right triangle?

Explain one step in long division.

What is the commutative property?

Illustrate why $\frac{1}{3}$ is greater than $\frac{1}{10}$.

What does the symbol "≈" mean?

What is a numerator?

How does a gram compare to a milligram?

What is the value of the digit 3 in the number 2.532?

Explain how to round 3,529 to the nearest thousand.

What does the term "congruent" mean?

What is the difference between five hundred six and five hundred and six tenths?

Journal Page Checklist — Teacher Copy

Student name: _____   Date: _____

Evaluated by: _____   Journal completed: ___ with assistance
                                                            ___ by self

- ❑ Student name is at the top.
- ❑ Date is at the top.
- ❑ Premise is written or neatly glued on the page.
- ❑ Illustration fits the premise.
- ❑ Illustration demonstrates understanding of premise.
- ❑ Illustration is neat and easy to understand.
- ❑ Illustration is labeled.
- ❑ Explanation answers the premise.
- ❑ Explanation refers to the illustration.
- ❑ Explanation is neat and easy to read.

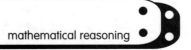

Journal Page Checklist — Student Copy

Student name: _____   Date: _____

Evaluated by: _____   Journal completed: ___ with assistance
                                                            ___ by self

- ❑ Student name is at the top.
- ❑ Date is at the top.
- ❑ Premise is written or neatly glued on the page.
- ❑ Illustration fits the premise.
- ❑ Illustration demonstrates understanding of premise.
- ❑ Illustration is neat and easy to understand.
- ❑ Illustration is labeled.
- ❑ Explanation answers the premise.
- ❑ Explanation refers to the illustration.
- ❑ Explanation is neat and easy to read.

Pay Attention

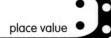

Write five different numbers that meet the criteria given.

1. A three-digit number whose digits add up to 9.

   _____ _____ _____ _____ _____

2. A six-digit even number whose digits have a sum of 13.

   _____ _____ _____ _____ _____

3. A four-digit odd number whose ones digit is half the hundreds digit.

   _____ _____ _____ _____ _____

4. A three-digit even number whose digits are larger from left to right.

   _____ _____ _____ _____ _____

5. A five-digit number with all odd digits. The digit in the thousands place is less than the digit in the hundreds place and the digit in the ones place.

   _____ _____ _____ _____ _____

6. A five-digit odd number whose digits add up to 15.

   _____ _____ _____ _____ _____

7. A six-digit even number. Each digit is different.

   _____ _____ _____ _____ _____

8. A four-digit even number with a digit less than 5 in the tens place and a digit greater than 5 in the thousands place.

   _____ _____ _____ _____ _____

9. A six-digit even number with 5 odd digits. The number is divisible by 2 and 10.

   _____ _____ _____ _____ _____

10. A five-digit odd number whose ten-thousands digit is twice the hundreds digit. Exactly one digit is repeated.

   _____ _____ _____ _____ _____

Change a Digit

Read the clue to write the four-digit number.
Change one digit each time to make the next statement true.

A. __ __ __ __   Write a four-digit number with all even digits that get smaller from left to right. The sum of the digits is 20.

B. __ __ __ __   This four-digit odd number has a hundreds digit that is one less than the ones digit.

C. __ __ __ __   This four-digit even number has ones and tens digits that are the same.

D. __ __ __ __   This four-digit odd number's digits have a sum of 21.

E. __ __ __ __   This four-digit odd number's thousands digit is twice that of the ones digit.

F. __ __ __ __   Each digit is one less than the digit to its left in this four-digit number.

G. __ __ __ __   Sixteen is the sum of the four digits in this odd number. The thousands and tens digits are equal.

H. __ __ __ __   The sum of this four-digit odd number's ones and tens digits is 10.

I. __ __ __ __   The sum of this four-digit even number's thousands and ones digits is 10.

J. __ __ __ __   This four-digit number has an odd thousands digit. This digit is also one half the ones digit.

K. __ __ __ __   This four-digit number has all odd digits that get larger from left to right.

Check your work.

1. Write the first number here. __ __ __ __

2. Reverse the order of the digits. __ __ __ __

3. Add one to each digit. __ __ __ __
   This is the number you ended with.

CD-4335 *Brain-Boosting Math*

: Numbers in the Box

Use the numbers in the box below to answer the questions.

| 42.15 | 389.1 | 2.59 | 91.17 | 827.20 | 4.43 |

1. Write the number that has a . . .
   a. 2 in the tens place _____
   b. 1 in the ones place _____
   c. 3 in the hundredths place _____
   d. 4 in the tens place _____
   e. 9 in the ones place _____
   f. 3 in the hundreds place _____
   g. 7 in the hundredths place _____
   h. 7 in the tens place _____

2. Find the minimum amount needed to make each number a whole number.
   a. 42.15 _____
   b. 389.1 _____
   c. 2.59 _____
   d. 91.17 _____
   e. 827.20 _____
   f. 4.43 _____

3. Even or odd?
   a. List the numbers with an even digit in the ones place. _____
   b. List the numbers with an odd digit in the tenths place. _____
   c. List the numbers with an odd digit in the tens place. _____

4. Put the numbers in order.
   a. From smallest to largest: _____ _____ _____ _____ _____ _____
   b. From largest to smallest: _____ _____ _____ _____ _____ _____

5. Choose four of the numbers. Write the standard and word form of each one.
   a. _____   _____
   b. _____   _____
   c. _____   _____
   d. _____   _____

6. Compare the numbers. Use each number at least once to make true comparisons.
   a. _____ > _____
   b. _____ < _____
   c. _____ < _____
   d. _____ = _____
   e. _____ > _____
   f. _____ > _____
   g. _____ < _____
   h. _____ = _____

7. Find the sum of all six numbers.

CD-4335 *Brain-Boosting Math*

: Higher or Lower?

Play the game Higher or Lower. Use the clues to find the number.

Example:

My number is between 2,600 and 8,900.

You are told that the number is greater than 2,600 but less than 8,900. Find the average of the two numbers and circle the guess that is closest to it. Circle 5,750 as the best guess.

Their average is _____5750_____ .

Guess: 3,000   (5,750)   8,000

Clue: lower

Now you know that the answer is lower than 5,750. You also know that it is higher than 2,600. Write the range and find the average. Continue the game.

A. It is between _____ and _____.
Their average is _____ .
Guess: 2,800   3,000   4,175
Clue: higher

B. It is between _____ and _____ .
Their average is _____ .
Guess: 4,960   5,500   5,700
Clue: lower

C. It is between _____ and _____ .
Their average is _____ .
Guess: 4,200   4,400   4,570
Clue: lower

D. It is between _____ and _____ .
Their average is _____ .
Guess: 4,370   4,450   4,500
Clue: lower

E. It is between _____ and _____ .
Their average is _____ .
Guess: 4,270   4,100   4,350
Clue: lower

F. It is between _____ and _____ .
Their average is _____ .
Guess: 4,190   4,220   4,260
Clue: higher

G. It is between _____ and _____ .
Their average is _____ .
Guess: 4,221   4,230   4,240
Clue: lower

H. It is between _____ and _____ .
Their average is _____ .
Guess: 4,230   4,235   4,239
Clue: lower

I. It is between _____ and _____ .
Their average is _____ .
Guess: 4,225   4,227   4,229
Clue: lower

J. It is between _____ and _____ .
Their average is _____ .
Guess: 4,220   4,221   4,223
Clue: higher

K. It is between _____ and _____ .

The number is [   ] .

Operating Room

Follow the order of operations to solve each problem. Working from left to right, begin inside the parentheses. Perform multiplication and division first. Then, do addition and subtraction.

A. 7 + 3 x 9 = _____

Rewrite so the answer is 90.

_____

B. (15 ÷ 5 + 4) x 2 = _____

Rewrite so the answer is 11.

_____

C. (6 + 30) ÷ (10 – 7) = _____

Rewrite so the answer is 2.

_____

D. 9 ÷ 3 + 12 ÷ 3 = _____

Rewrite so the answer is 5.

_____

E. (1 + 3) x (11 – 5) = _____

Rewrite so the answer is 29.

_____

F. 21 ÷ 3 + 1 x 6 = _____

Rewrite so the answer is 48.

_____

G. 25 x (2 – 2) x 12 = _____

Rewrite so the answer is 26.

_____

Write a number sentence for each of the following answers using the order of operations and these numbers: 5, 5, 5, and 5.

H. _____ = 7

I. _____ = 6

J. _____ = 10

K. _____ = 130

L. _____ = 3

Write a number sentence for each of the following answers using the order of operations and these numbers: 3, 4, 5, 6, 7.

M. _____ = 13

N. _____ = 75

O. _____ = 3

P. _____ = 17

Q. _____ = 15

CD-4335 *Brain-Boosting Math*

Roman Numerals

Look at the number written in standard form. Circle the correct Roman numeral.

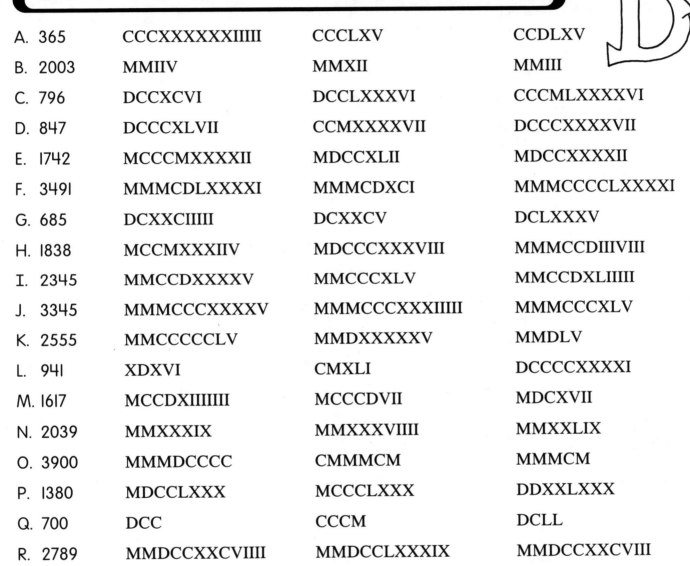

I = 1	V = 5	X = 10	L = 50	C = 100	D = 500	M = 1000

A. 365   CCCXXXXXIIIII   CCCLXV   CCDLXV

B. 2003   MMIIV   MMXII   MMIII

C. 796   DCCXCVI   DCCLXXXVI   CCCMLXXXXVI

D. 847   DCCCXLVII   CCMXXXXVII   DCCCXXXXVII

E. 1742   MCCCMXXXXII   MDCCXLII   MDCCXXXXII

F. 3491   MMMCDLXXXXI   MMMCDXCI   MMMCCCCLXXXXI

G. 685   DCXXCIIIII   DCXXCV   DCLXXXV

H. 1838   MCCMXXXIIV   MDCCCXXXVIII   MMMCCDIIIVIII

I. 2345   MMCCDXXXXV   MMCCCXLV   MMCCDXLIIIII

J. 3345   MMMCCCXXXXV   MMMCCCXXXIIIII   MMMCCCXLV

K. 2555   MMCCCCLV   MMDXXXXV   MMDLV

L. 941   XDXVI   CMXLI   DCCCCXXXXI

M. 1617   MCCDXIIIIII   MCCCDVII   MDCXVII

N. 2039   MMXXXIX   MMXXXVIIII   MMXXLIX

O. 3900   MMMDCCCC   CMMMCM   MMMCM

P. 1380   MDCCLXXX   MCCCLXXX   DDXXLXXX

Q. 700   DCC   CCCM   DCLL

R. 2789   MMDCCXXCVIIII   MMDCCLXXXIX   MMDCCXXCVIII

Choose three Roman numerals from above. Use each in a sentence.

Example: There are CCCLXV days in one year.

1. _____

2. _____

3. _____

Name _____

Inventions

Circle the Roman numeral in each fact. Rewrite the number as a standard number to find the year of each of these mathematical inventions.

| I = 1   V = 5   X = 10   L = 50   C = 100   D = 500   M = 1000 |

A. Gabriel Fahrenheit invented the mercury thermometer in MDCCXIV. _____ ( )

B. The abacus was invented in China around CDXCIX B.C. _____ ( )

C. From MDCLXV to MDCLXXV calculus was independently invented by two men, Sir Isaac Newton from England and Gottfried Leibniz from Germany. _____ ( )

D. The digital calculating machine was invented in MDCCCXXIII by Charles Babbage of England. _____ ( )

E. Algebra was invented by Diophantus about CCL in Greece. _____ ( )

F. The pendulum clock was invented in the Netherlands in MDCLVI by Christian Huygens. _____ ( )

G. Logarithms were invented in MDCXIV by John Napier from Scotland. _____ ( )

H. The cash register was invented in the United States in MDCCCLXXIX by James Ritty. _____ ( )

I. Rene Descartes from France invented coordinate geometry in MDCXXXVII. _____ ( )

J. The theory of numbers was invented in MDCXL by Frenchman Pierre de Fermat. _____ ( )

K. Blaise Pascal of France invented the calculating machine in MDCXLII. _____ ( )

L. In MMDC B.C., geometry was invented in Egypt. _____ ( )

M. The Italian Galileo invented the thermometer in MDXCIII. _____ ( )

N. The calendar was invented in Babylon around DCXCIX B.C. _____ ( )

O. The chronometer was invented in MDCCXXXV by John Harrison of England. _____ ( )

Put the inventions in order from earliest to most recent. Write the numbers 1–15 in the boxes.

CD-4335 *Brain-Boosting Math*

Charting Roman Numerals

Roman numerals/place value/basic operations

Fill in the chart. In the fourth column, write a number sentence using standard numbers. Include subtraction, addition, multiplication, and division problems. In the last column, rewrite the problem using Roman numerals.

I = 1   V = 5   X = 10   L = 50   C = 100   D = 500   M = 1000

Roman Numeral	Standard Form	Expanded Form	Number Sentence Standard Numerals	Roman Numerals
	9			
	22			
	574			
	46			
	93			
	2,418			
CDIX				
XXXVI				
CMLXXIV				
MMDCIX				
DCCXLVII				
XCIX				
		3000 + 400 + 30 + 9		
		300 + 90 + 2		
		50 + 6		
		2000 + 400 + 30 + 9		
		900 + 10 + 8		
		1000 + 700 + 80 + 4		

Choose two Roman numerals from the table. Draw or stamp their representational forms below.

A.

B.

CD-4335 *Brain-Boosting Math*

Roman Time

Match the time on each clock with the digital form written in Roman numerals.
Rewrite the time using standard numbers.

| I = 1 | V = 5 | X = 10 | L = 50 |

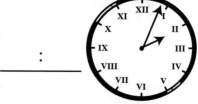

___ : ___

Roman Times

II:IV

V:LVI

VII:VII

V:XXII

X:XXXIV

IX:VIII

I:XLIX

XII:XLIX

VI:LIV

III:XXIX

VIII:LI

XI:XXXVIII

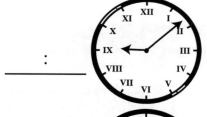

___ : ___

___ : ___

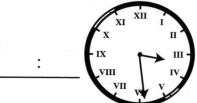

___ : ___

___ : ___

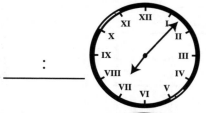

___ : ___

___ : ___

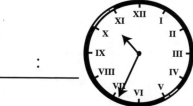

___ : ___

___ : ___

___ : ___

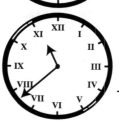

___ : ___

Way Big Amusement Park

Gobie's family is planning a visit to Way Big Amusement Park. The park opens at 9:00 a.m. and closes at 8 p.m. Gobie's house is 150 miles away from the park. Plan the visit.

Include the following activities:

- wake up / get ready
- leave house
- travel time / activities in car
- breakfast, lunch, and dinner
- arrive at park
- stand in admission line
- rides (at least 3)
- shows (at least 1)
- visit gift shop

Way Big Amusement Park Family Schedule		
Activity	Length of Time	Start and Stop Times
leave park	10 minutes	8:00 – 8:10

CD-4335 *Brain-Boosting Math*

Name _____

According to the sleep chart, students who are between six and twelve years old should get 9 to 11 hours of sleep each night.

Ten student sleep times are recorded in the chart. The chart includes the time to bed and the time up. Determine how long each student slept. Record it in the chart. For the next nine rows, write the times you and eight other classmates went to bed and got up.

Name	Time to Bed	Time Up	Time in Bed
Jesma	9:30	7:30	
Sirdo	9:00	6:30	
Judy	8:45	7:30	
Dillon	9:00	7:00	
Melina	10:00	6:30	
Jen	9:30	7:45	
Rebecca	9:15	6:30	
Omarha	10:00	7:45	
Sydney	11:00	7:00	
Armani	10:30	7:30	

Record the data on a graph showing the number of hours the students slept. Label the graph. Write three statements supported by the information you collected and graphed.

1. _____

2. _____

3. _____

Name _____

Meg, Ian, and Jill are playing Card Golf. The game is played with several decks of cards. There are nine hands, or rounds, per game. Each player receives six cards in a round, two at a time. Calculate the scores to determine the winner.

Scoring Rules

Adjacent cards with same value = 0 points	King = 0 points
Adjacent aces = subtract 4 points	Jack or queen = 10 points
Ace = subtract 2 points	Number cards = face value

Meg   Ian   Jill   Meg   Ian   Jill   Meg   Ian   Jill

Hand 1:

9 2 ___	7 3 ___	A K ___
A K ___	4 4 ___	J J ___
5 4 ___	A 2 ___	A 2 ___

Total: ___   Total: ___   Total: ___

Hand 2:

K A ___	8 8 ___	K 3 ___
6 5 ___	A 7 ___	A K ___
2 2 ___	Q A ___	2 2 ___

Total: ___   Total: ___   Total: ___
Running   Running   Running
total: ___   total: ___   total: ___

Hand 3:

9 2 ___	K A ___	10 10 ___
4 4 ___	7 7 ___	K A ___
K A ___	J J ___	3 4 ___

Total: ___   Total: ___   Total: ___
Running   Running   Running
total: ___   total: ___   total: ___

Hand 4:

4 4 ___	Q Q ___	3 3 ___
K K ___	4 7 ___	A A ___
2 2 ___	K 9 ___	9 5 ___

Total: ___   Total: ___   Total: ___
Running   Running   Running
total: ___   total: ___   total: ___

Hand 5:

A A ___	2 2 ___	A K ___
2 K ___	3 3 ___	9 9 ___
8 8 ___	A 2 ___	4 K ___

Total: ___   Total: ___   Total: ___
Running   Running   Running
total: ___   total: ___   total: ___

Hand 6:

2 3 ___	A 2 ___	2 5 ___
A 7 ___	A K ___	7 7 ___
2 4 ___	4 5 ___	K K ___

Total: ___   Total: ___   Total: ___
Running   Running   Running
total: ___   total: ___   total: ___

Hand 7:

2 K ___	K A ___	6 6 ___
A K ___	8 9 ___	10 10 ___
A K ___	2 4 ___	K A ___

Total: ___   Total: ___   Total: ___
Running   Running   Running
total: ___   total: ___   total: ___

Hand 8:

2 2 ___	5 5 ___	4 4 ___
A A ___	K 2 ___	2 3 ___
K A ___	J J ___	K A ___

Total: ___   Total: ___   Total: ___
Running   Running   Running
total: ___   total: ___   total: ___

Hand 9:

A K ___	8 8 ___	K 2 ___
5 K ___	4 5 ___	3 K ___
2 2 ___	10 10 ___	A A ___

Total: ___   Total: ___   Total: ___
Running   Running   Running
total: ___   total: ___   total: ___

The player with the lowest score wins. Who won? _____

Algebra Challenge

addition and subtraction/algebra/mathematical reasoning

Solve to find the value of each variable. All variables are less than 10.

$c = y + e$

$y - q = u$

$e + e + e = c$

$u = q + q$

$u + q = c - e$

$c = 9$ $u = \boxed{}$

$e = \boxed{}$ $y = \boxed{}$

$q = \boxed{}$

$o + w = x + z$

$x + w = o - w$

$z + z = o + x + w$

$w + w + x = o$

$o - x + w = z$

$z = w + w + w$

$o = \boxed{}$ $x = \boxed{}$

$w = \boxed{}$ $z = 6$

$t + s = p + p$

$j + j = t - s$

$t = p + j$

$p + s = t - s - s$

$j + s = p$

$j = \boxed{}$ $s = \boxed{}$

$p = 4$ $t = \boxed{}$

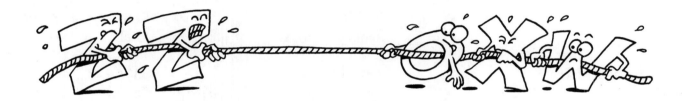

$f + f = b$

$k + f = g$

$k = b + f$

$b + f + f = g$

$g - f = b + f$

$b = 4$ $g = \boxed{}$

$f = \boxed{}$ $k = \boxed{}$

$m + h + r = d$

$a = d - h$

$m + r = a$

$m = r + h$

$d = m + m$

$h + h = r$

$a = \boxed{}$ $h = \boxed{}$

$d = \boxed{}$ $m = \boxed{}$

$r = 2$

$v = d + l$

$n + n + n = l$

$i - l = l + d$

$l + v = i$

$i - n = v + d$

$d = \boxed{}$ $n = \boxed{}$

$i = \boxed{}$ $v = \boxed{}$

$l = 3$

CD-4335 *Brain-Boosting Math*

Those Romans!

addition and subtraction with regrouping/Roman numerals

Change the Roman numerals to standard numbers. Write the problem vertically and solve. Rewrite the answer using Roman numerals.

I = 1   V = 5   X = 10   L = 50   C = 100   D = 500   M = 1000

1. CXXIX + CLXXX

2. CDI – CCLI

3. DCI – CDXVII

4. CDLXXVII + CCLXXIX

5. CCLXXXIV + CCCVIII

6. DXCI – CLXIII

7. CCCXCI + CLIX

8. CMXXXII – DLV

9. CCXVI + DCLXVIII

10. CMXXVI – CCXIX

11. DCCXXVI + CCXLIX

12. CCCLXXXIV – LXXVII

 Values

Write the value of the underlined digit.

A. 3<u>5</u>4,782 _____

B. 5,290,8<u>1</u>3 _____

C. 724,36<u>2</u> _____

D. 6<u>7</u>,489 _____

E. <u>2</u>12,472 _____

F. 2,400,2<u>7</u>5 _____

G. 10<u>2</u>,557 _____

H. 3,453,6<u>1</u>2 _____

I. <u>4</u>72,371 _____

J. 61,27<u>8</u> _____

K. 3<u>6</u>2,727 _____

L. 1,160,<u>3</u>64 _____

M. <u>6</u>21,290 _____

N. <u>1</u>5,258 _____

O. 6,517,29<u>3</u> _____

P. 901,0<u>0</u>3 _____

Q. 142,6<u>2</u>7 _____

R. 52<u>1</u>,618 _____

Add the values to make a standard number.

S. Answers A–F

T. Answers G–L

U. Answers M–R

Write the equations vertically. Use the values from S, T, and U above to find each sum.

1. S + S

2. S + T

3. S + U

4. T + U

5. U + U

6. S + T + U

Write the sums from problems 1–3 as expanded numbers.

7. S + S _____

8. S + T _____

9. S + U _____

Cross Patch

Add. Use your answers to complete each grid.

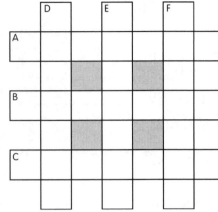

Across

A.　2631448
　　　749213
　　4930406
　　　　2781
　　+　198364

B.　　463951
　　　293466
　　1889423
　　　　7992
　　+　36483

C.　3526808
　　　　9426
　　1745971
　　1268319
　　+　174550

Down

D.　2331403
　　　566987
　　　26825
　　1009743
　　+　631618

E.　　486092
　　1645357
　　　7806
　　2492534
　　+ 1629865

F.　　48932
　　2192443
　　707527
　　145869
　　+　6403

Across

A.　　45736
　　2603481
　　826018
　　3469752
　　+　6435

B.　7062495
　　　93246
　　528793
　　1844631
　　+　264868

C.　4625191
　　2930467
　　298154
　　1008479
　　+　64827

Down

Write three addition problems with five addends each.
The sums must fit in the puzzle.

D.　　　　　　E.　　　　　　F.

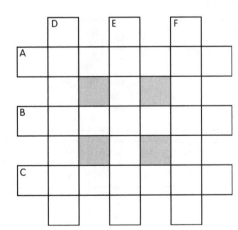

　　　　　　CD-4335 *Brain-Boosting Math*

Addition Boxes

This strategy can be used with any size addition problem. The difference in this strategy is where the regrouping takes place. It takes place below the equal sign rather than above the first addend.

1. Make a box below each place (ones, tens, hundreds, etc.).
2. Make a diagonal line from the top right to the bottom left of each box.
   Above the line is the next place. Below the line is the place of that column.

Example:

```
      7 8 4 5 5 6
  +   4 8 5 3 4 7
    ┌─┬─┬─┬─┬─┬─┐
    │1│1│9│8│①│1│
    │/1│/6│/9│/8│/9│/3│
    └─┴─┴─┴─┴─┴─┘
  1 2 6 9 9 0 3
```

Draw the addition boxes. Add the numbers in each place and write the sum in the box. Shade each diagonal value with a different color: ones yellow, tens pink, and so on. Write the sums of the diagonals below the boxes. Regroup to the next place when needed.

A.
```
      6 5 4 9
  +   7 3 7 2
```

B.
```
      5 4 9 8
  +   4 6 7 2
```

C.
```
      6 5 4 6
  +   2 7 9 7
```

D.
```
      3 1 6 8
  +   5 7 3 8
```

E.
```
      7 6 4 9 2 5
  +   1 8 9 3 4 2
```

F.
```
      2 7 4 1 7 3
  +   4 8 9 2 5 6
```

G.
```
      2 3 1 1 7 4
  +   5 8 2 9 6 8
```

H.
```
      3 8 9 4 4 2
  +   9 5 8 3 1 8
```

I.
```
      4 1 8 3 6 0
  +     6 2 7 5 3
```

Try two more addition problems of your own using addition boxes. Check your answers with a calculator. Explain why addition boxes work.

_____

_____

More Addition Boxes

addition strategy/multiple addends

The addition box strategy can also be used with multiple addends.

1. Make a box below each place (ones, tens, hundreds, etc.).
2. Make a diagonal line from the top right to the bottom left of each box. Above the line is the next place. Below the line is the place of that column.

Example:

```
    6  2  4  6  9
    7  3  2  6  7
 +  3  5  6  2  7
 _____
  /1 /1 /1 /  /2
 / 6/ 0/ 2/4 / 3
  1  7  1  3  6  3
```

Draw the addition boxes. Add the numbers in each place and write the sum in the box. Shade each diagonal value with a different color: ones yellow, tens pink, and so on. Write the sums of the diagonals below the boxes. Regroup to the next place when needed.

A.
```
    7  5  3  2  9  8
    1  2  8  4  5  1
 +  4  5  5  8  2  9
```

B.
```
    1  9  2  4  4  6
    3  9  6  5  6  3
 +  4  7  7  4  3  5
```

C.
```
    6  2  8  3  0  6
    8  3  8  9  3  2
 +  4  6  1  6  2  6
```

D.
```
    2  7  3  7  2  8
    9  5  3  9  3  8
 +  4  1  6  7  2  8
```

E.
```
       2  8  0  9
          4  6  5
       5  2  9  4
    5  6  8  9  3
          8  1  1
    5  1  3  8  2
 +     3  0  3  8
```

F.
```
    5  5  6  7  8
    2  8  6  9
    5  6  2  9
    8  3  1  1
       6  3  2
    3  1  2  8
 +     7  4  6
```

G.
```
       6  2  7  2
       4  1  1  8
          9  2  6
    2  1  7  2  1
    6  2  0  0  6
       1  7  0  4
 +     2  6  8  1
```

H.
```
    7  8  9  2  5  6
          3  7  6  5
    2  4  5  7  8  9
          2  0  8  7
    8  0  4  2  7  7
 +        4  8  5
```

Try two more problems of your own. Check your answers with a calculator.

CD-4335 *Brain-Boosting Math*

Missing Digits

addition and subtraction with regrouping/mathematical reasoning

Add or subtract. Find the missing digits.

A.
```
  5 7 □ 8 3 □
+ □ 7 4 □ 3 6
───────────
1 2 □ 1 7 □ 8
```

B.
```
  □ 3 7 1 □ □
+ 8 6 □ 5 9 3
───────────
1 1 □ 0 □ 8 7
```

C.
```
  □ 6 3 □ 5 □
- 4 8 □ 4 9 3
───────────
2 □ 0 0 □ 8
```

D.
```
  4 9 2 □ 6 9
- □ 5 □ 1 7 □
───────────
2 □ 5 8 □ 4
```

E.
```
  □ □ 0 7 0 □
- 2 3 □ □ 4 3
───────────
3 2 0 8 □ 9
```

F.
```
  □ 3 2 5 6 8
+ 5 □ □ □ □ 5
───────────
1 5 1 2 8 4 □
```

G.
```
  5 4 1 □ □ □
+ 1 □ □ 6 7 9
───────────
□ 7 1 5 5 1
```

H.
```
  1 6 □ 0 9 1
- 1 □ 8 3 □ □
───────────
□ 3 1 □ 2 7
```

I.
```
  7 □ □ 8 □ 6
- □ 8 2 7 4 □
───────────
5 4 2 □ 7 7
```

J.
```
  □ 9 □ 7 2 6
+ 3 □ 2 1 9 □
───────────
8 7 7 □ □ 3
```

K.
```
  2 6 4 □ □ 0
- 1 □ 4 6 9 □
───────────
□ 2 □ 4 6 8
```

L.
```
  3 □ 9 4 □ 6
+ □ 9 3 □ 8 5
───────────
6 8 □ 3 4 □
```

M.
```
  4 4 □ 0 □ □
- 2 7 3 □ 8 4
───────────
□ □ 9 8 2 9
```

N.
```
  □ 0 0 2 0 1
- 3 1 □ 3 □ 6
───────────
1 □ 5 □ 5 □
```

O.
```
  9 0 □ 4 □ 0
- 3 □ 2 6 4 □
───────────
□ 6 3 □ 8 8
```

P.
```
    3 □ 9 2 5 □
    □ 2 6 4 8 3
+     1 1 □ 5 6 2
───────────
  □ 0 1 9 □ □ 8
```

Q.
```
    3 7 □ □ 3 0
    1 5 2 8 □ □
+ 2 □ 3 6 4 4
───────────
  □ 3 3 0 2 1
```

R.
```
    4 8 4 □ 8 5
    7 □ 3 1 5 4
+   6 2 □ 6 □ □
───────────
  □ □ 3 5 6 1 2
```

CD-4335 *Brain-Boosting Math*

Missing Digits (continued)

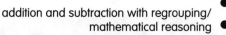

addition and subtraction with regrouping/
mathematical reasoning

Make your own six-digit addition and subtraction problems.
Check for accuracy with a calculator.

A.

B.

C.

D.

E.

F.

G.

H.

I.

Copy your problems into the boxes below. Leave the shaded boxes blank.
Fold the paper back along the fold line. Trade with a friend.

fold

Add or subtract. Find the missing digits. When you are done, open the page to check your work.

A.

B.

C.

D.

E.

F.

G.

H.

I.

Thermometer

multi-addend addition

The first thermometer was invented in 1593 by Galileo Galilei. Solve the problems. Then, follow the directions below to find out who made the next improvement on the thermometer.

1
```
    35623
  2354782
+ 6342627
```

2
```
   946536
    83970
+ 8439233
```

3
```
   845732
  5889453
+ 4366534
```

4
```
  5477543
    34523
+  621334
```

5
```
  2394998
  4346234
+  123526
```

6
```
   735528
  3381545
+   38116
```

7
```
   867426
  2475922
+ 3406801
```

8
```
    78921
  5934602
+  848773
```

9
```
   938856
    77658
+  374554
```

10
```
  3245623
   675556
+   53454
```

11
```
   483962
  2416375
+  344263
```

12
```
  1552124
  4462719
+  297234
```

Underline the three thousands digits (thousands, ten thousands, and hundred thousands) in each answer and find that number in the code. Then circle the next three digits in each answer. Find that number in the key below. Use the key to write the name of the German who invented the mercury thermometer in 1714.

Code:

862	750	312	155	244	733	133
___	___	___	___	___	___	___

101	750	391	155	733	974	391	733	244	864
___	___	___	___	___	___	___	___	___	___

Key

A = 149, 732	B = 077, 139	E = 032, 123	F = 719, 919
G = 296, 739	H = 068, 964	I = 600, 422	L = 400, 198
N = 633, 120	R = 189, 962	T = 758, 140	

CD-4335 *Brain-Boosting Math*

Hourglass

addition and subtraction/mathematical reasoning

Start at the bottom of the large hourglass. Add adjacent numbers. Write the sum in the space above the addends. Continue until you reach the center of the hourglass. Then, change the operation. Subtract until you reach the top. Some numbers are included to help you along.

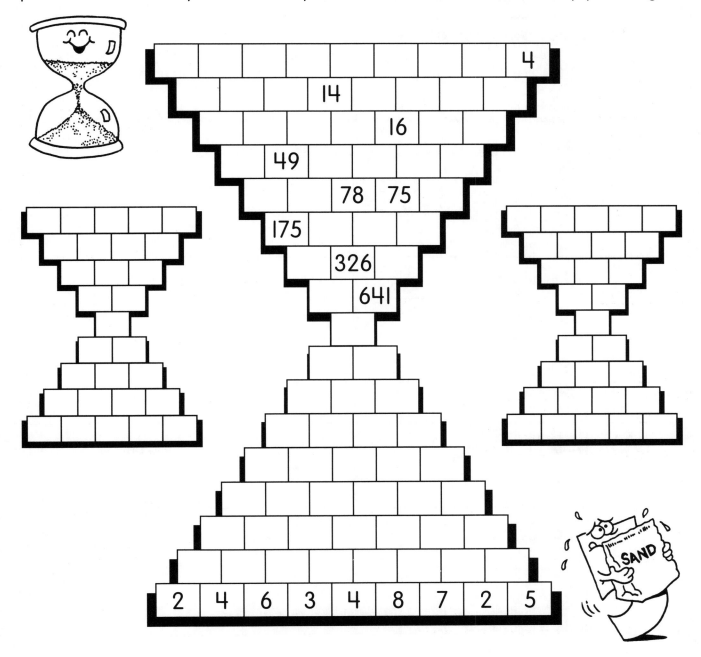

Challenge: Fill in the smaller hourglasses. No rows can be identical. Zeros are only allowed in the top and bottom rows. Each number in these two rows must be less than 15.

CD-4335 *Brain-Boosting Math*

Give It a Loan

subtraction/alternate strategy to regrouping

When subtraction problems require regrouping, try giving them a loan instead. Just add the same amount to both numbers to bring the bottom number up to the next ten or hundred. The difference remains the same. Look at the examples below.

Regrouping needed in the ones place			Regrouping needed in the tens place		
91 − 49 42	Add 1 to both.	92 − 50 42	245 − 193 52	Add 10 to both.	255 − 203 52

Solve each problem. Then, use the loan strategy and solve again. Compare your answers.

A. 756
    − 348   Add 2 to both.   758
                                       − 350

B. 961
    − 198   Add 2 to both.   963
                                       − 200

C. 647
    − 266   Add 40 to both.   687
                                       − 306

D. 572
    − 365   Add 5 to both.

E. 648
    − 291   Add 10 to both.

F. 626
    − 243   Add 60 to both.

G. 851
    − 327   Add ____ to both.

H. 935
    − 855   Add ____ to both.

I. 614
    − 263   Add ____ to both.

LOANS →

Explain why this strategy works. _____

_____

Does this strategy work with other place value locations?
Try it with these problems: 3,284 − 1,421   71,538 − 45,207   736,859 − 271,636

CD-4335 *Brain-Boosting Math*

Multiple Loans

subtraction/alternate strategy to regrouping

You have learned to loan the same amount to both numbers in a subtraction problem. It is also possible to give multiple loans. Just give one loan at a time.

When regrouping is needed in both the tens and ones places, give two loans in two steps.

Example:					
$\begin{array}{r} 536 \\ -289 \\ \hline 247 \end{array}$	Add 1 to both.	$\begin{array}{r} 537 \\ -290 \\ \hline 247 \end{array}$	Then, add 10 to both.	$\begin{array}{r} 547 \\ -300 \\ \hline 247 \end{array}$

Solve each problem. Then, use the loan strategy and solve again. Compare your answers.

A. $\begin{array}{r} 952 \\ -478 \\ \hline \end{array}$ Add 2 to both. $\begin{array}{r} 954 \\ -480 \\ \hline \end{array}$ Add 20 to both. $\begin{array}{r} 974 \\ -500 \\ \hline \end{array}$

B. $\begin{array}{r} 707 \\ -488 \\ \hline \end{array}$ Add 2 to both. $\begin{array}{r} 709 \\ -490 \\ \hline \end{array}$ Add 10 to both. $\begin{array}{r} 719 \\ -500 \\ \hline \end{array}$

C. $\begin{array}{r} 321 \\ -255 \\ \hline \end{array}$ Add _____ to both.   Add _____ to both.

D. $\begin{array}{r} 432 \\ -279 \\ \hline \end{array}$ Add _____ to both.   Add _____ to both.

E. $\begin{array}{r} 3701 \\ -546 \\ \hline \end{array}$ Add _____ to both.   Add _____ to both.

F. $\begin{array}{r} 9932 \\ -5864 \\ \hline \end{array}$ Add _____ to both.   Add _____ to both.

G. $\begin{array}{r} 9365 \\ -8628 \\ \hline \end{array}$ Add _____ to both.   Add _____ to both.

H. $\begin{array}{r} 5632 \\ -1585 \\ \hline \end{array}$ Add _____ to both.   Add _____ to both.

   CD-4335 *Brain-Boosting Math*

Zero Land

Zeros are zapping every spaceship that comes along. Find each difference.

A. 80000
  − 34502

B. 20000
  − 16241

C. 50000
  − 25367

D. 70000
  − 32569

E. 100000
  − 52634

F. 600000
  − 324806

G. 500000
  − 162398

H. 400000
  − 237945

I. 701101
  − 523342

J. 902003
  − 325891

K. 300201
  − 132473

L. 801010
  − 425622

Many ships found safety by hiding in the craters of the moon above Zero Land. Go back and add 999 to each of your answers. Then, find those new sums in the craters below. Shade each crater that contains one of your final sums.

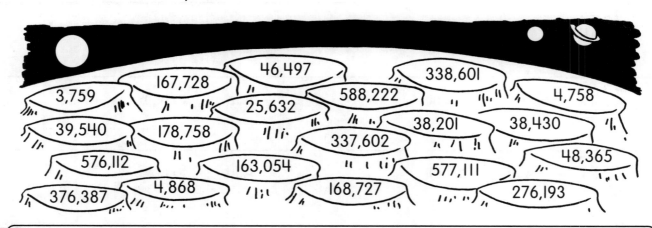

Make That Number

Read the given number. Think of a number sentence whose ANSWER is that number. Write the number sentence. Think of more number sentences. Write each on a new line. Use addition, subtraction, multiplication, and division. Construct a problem that uses the order of operations. You may add more number sentences on the back of this sheet or another paper.

99

5

24

110

50

36

144

246

Compare your answers with a partner. Put a check mark next to the number sentences you both have. Circle the ones that only you have.

Color by Number

Solve the problems. Check your answers. Use your answers and the key to color the picture.

> green = 0–3   brown = 4–6   orange = 7–9   pink = 10–15   blue = 16–22
>
> yellow = 23–34   purple = 35–45   red = 46–60   black = 61–90

Color by Number (continued)

Create your own color-by-number picture.

1. Draw a picture in the space below.
2. Choose 5–12 colors to use in the picture.
3. Assign a range of answers to each color. For example, 12–20 = red. Use the ranges to write a color code across the top or bottom of the page.
4. Decide what types of numbers to use on your worksheet: whole numbers, fractions, decimals, or mixed numbers.

5. Decide what color each section or part of the picture should be. Then, write a multiplication or division problem for each part with an answer that fits in the range. For example, if answers 20–30 are black, write the problem **5 x 5 =** inside a tire. Continue until every space has a problem.
6. Outline everything with a black marker.
7. Trade with a partner.

Fooling You

Write each expression to fill in the missing parts of the table.

Algebraic Expression	Expression in Words
	nine less than g
	k divided by five
	v and five
	y decreased by seven
	six times s
	twelve divided by j
	t less than fifteen
	twenty more than c
$12e$	
$w + 34$	
$36 \div m$	
$q - 6$	
$n - 3$	
$7z$	
$17 + f$	

Solve the expressions for each given value. Use another sheet of paper to show your work.

$5t$

t	Answer
3	
90	
22	
500	
15	

$10,200 - m$

m	Answer
6,328	
9,004	
2,561	
3,264	
10,133	

$1,500 \div j$

j	Answer
50	
2	
25	
14	
32	

$x + 97,846$

x	Answer
26,423	
84,532	
36,274	
57,647	
14,925	

CD-4335 *Brain-Boosting Math*

Arrangement

basic operations/problem solving

Arrange each group of numbers in the boxes to arrive at the correct answer.
Apply each function in the order given.

A. ☐ ÷ ☐ × ☐ ÷ ☐ − ☐ × ☐ = 10   2, 3, 4, 5, 6, 12

B. ☐ + ☐ ÷ ☐ × ☐ − ☐ ÷ ☐ = 3   1, 3, 5, 6, 8, 9

C. ☐ + ☐ + ☐ ÷ ☐ × ☐ + ☐ = 5   1, 2, 3, 5, 7, 7

D. ☐ + ☐ ÷ ☐ × ☐ + ☐ ÷ ☐ = 5   2, 3, 4, 5, 7, 8

E. ☐ × ☐ − ☐ ÷ ☐ × ☐ + ☐ ÷ ☐ = 3   1, 2, 3, 4, 5, 7, 9

F. ☐ × ☐ − ☐ ÷ ☐ + ☐ × ☐ ÷ ☐ = 3   2, 3, 4, 5, 7, 8, 9

Using only the numbers in the box, write one number sentence to equal each answer below.
Apply each function in the order written. Use all nine numbers each time.

G. **11** =

H. **12** =

I. **2** =

1	2	3
4	5	6
7	8	9

Use five numbers to write your own number sentence chain. Write the chain in the top set of boxes below. Then, copy the chain again, leaving out the numbers but including the function symbols. List the numbers used. Trade with a partner.

Key:

☐ ○ ☐ ○ ☐ ○ ☐ = ☐   ____, ____, ____, ____

fold

Partner:

☐ ○ ☐ ○ ☐ ○ ☐ = ☐   ____, ____, ____, ____

CD-4335 *Brain-Boosting Math*

Back and Forth

multiplication/Roman numerals

| I = 1 | V = 5 | X = 10 | L = 50 |
| C = 100 | D = 500 | M = 1000 | |

Write the Roman numeral for each standard number.

A. 2456 _____   B. 894 _____

C. 628 _____   D. 1406 _____

E. 3050 _____   F. 69 _____

G. 2247 _____   H. 3444 _____

Multiply. Rewrite each answer as a Roman numeral.

| I. 35
x 56 | J. 92
x 28 | K. 71
x 49 | L. 346
x 5 | M. 425
x 7 | N. 627
x 4 |

Write the standard form of each Roman numeral.

1. CDLXV _____   2. MMDXXX _____

3. MDCXLII _____   4. XCIX _____

5. MMMCLXII _____   6. CCLVII _____

7. MMDCCCLXXXVIII _____   8. MXXXIV _____

9. MV _____   10. MMMCDXCIII _____

11. What is the largest Roman numeral? _____

12. Write five standard numbers on the lines. Write the correct Roman numeral below each one.

_____ _____ _____ _____ _____

_____ _____ _____ _____ _____

Place-Value Drawing

multiplication strategy

One way to solve multiplication problems is to visualize the numbers. This strategy uses place-value drawings in a grid format.

Represent the numbers as shown here:

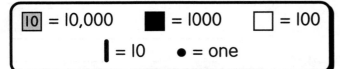

$\boxed{10}$ = 10,000	$\blacksquare$ = 1000	$\square$ = 100
$|$ = 10	$\bullet$ = one	

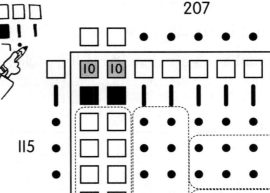

Example: 115 x 207 = 23,805

Set up the grid as shown. Place the first number vertically along the side. Place the second number horizontally across the top. Multiply and draw the products in the intersections between the two numbers. Group and count the representations inside the grid to find your answer.

Solve the problems on another piece of paper. Attach the paper and record your answers here.

A.   1351
     x   7

= ____ ten thousands, ____ thousands, ____ hundreds, ____ tens, ____ ones

B.   262
      x 32

= ____ ten thousands, ____ thousands, ____ hundreds, ____ tens, ____ ones

C.   19
      x 54

= ____ ten thousands, ____ thousands, ____ hundreds, ____ tens, ____ ones

D.   423
     x 215

= ____ ten thousands, ____ thousands, ____ hundreds, ____ tens, ____ ones

Explain why you can find the correct product using this strategy.

_____

CD-4335 *Brain-Boosting Math*

Breaking Apart

One multiplication strategy involves breaking the problem into parts.

Example: 34 x 52 can be written as (4 x 2) + (4 x 50) + (30 x 2) + (30 x 50)

Break apart each problem. Write the multiplication sentences that make up each problem. Solve and add. The sum is the product.

SNAP

A.   7 5
  x 2 9

___ x ___ = ___
___ x ___ = ___
___ x ___ = ___
___ x ___ = + ___

B.   9 2
  x 3 3

___ x ___ = ___
___ x ___ = ___
___ x ___ = ___
___ x ___ = + ___

C.   3 5
  x 2 6

___ x ___ = ___
___ x ___ = ___
___ x ___ = ___
___ x ___ = + ___

D.   1 6 2 0
  x   9

___ x ___ = ___
___ x ___ = ___
___ x ___ = ___
___ x ___ = + ___

E.   2 5 6 1
  x   4

___ x ___ = ___
___ x ___ = ___
___ x ___ = ___
___ x ___ = + ___

F.   4 0 5 9
  x   6

___ x ___ = ___
___ x ___ = ___
___ x ___ = ___
___ x ___ = + ___

G.   5 4 7
  x   3 2

___ x ___ = ___
___ x ___ = ___
___ x ___ = ___
___ x ___ = ___
___ x ___ = ___
___ x ___ = + ___

H.   3 3 3
  x   1 4

___ x ___ = ___
___ x ___ = ___
___ x ___ = ___
___ x ___ = ___
___ x ___ = ___
___ x ___ = + ___

Try these additional problems on the back of this page.

    5 6 1   3 4 0   6 3 8   7 3 8
  x   1 3   x 1 5 3   x 4 6 9   x 1 1 1

CD-4335 *Brain-Boosting Math*

Name _____

Another multiplication strategy involves breaking the problem into just two or three parts.

Example: 34 x 52 can also be written as (4 x 52) + (30 x 52)

Break each problem into two or three simpler problems. Write the multiplication
sentences that make up each problem. Solve and add. The sum is the product.

I. 56
   x 27
   ___ x ___ = ____
   ___ x ___ = ___ +
   _____

J. 85
   x 71
   ___ x ___ = ____
   ___ x ___ = ___ +
   _____

K. 69
   x 13
   ___ x ___ = ____
   ___ x ___ = ___ +
   _____

L. 46
   x 38
   ___ x ___ = ____
   ___ x ___ = ___ +
   _____

M. 243
   x 61
   ___ x ___ = ____
   ___ x ___ = ____
   ___ x ___ = ___ +
   _____

N. 156
   x 26
   ___ x ___ = ____
   ___ x ___ = ____
   ___ x ___ = ___ +
   _____

O. 422
   x 57
   ___ x ___ = ____
   ___ x ___ = ____
   ___ x ___ = ___ +
   _____

P. 854
   x 14
   ___ x ___ = ____
   ___ x ___ = ____
   ___ x ___ = ___ +
   _____

Q. 625
   x 138
   ___ x ___ = ____
   ___ x ___ = ____
   ___ x ___ = ___ +
   _____

R. 709
   x 483
   ___ x ___ = ____
   ___ x ___ = ____
   ___ x ___ = ___ +
   _____

Explain why you can find the correct product using this strategy.

_____

Use the place-value drawing strategy to solve one problem from this page.
Then, use the original breaking-apart strategy on a different problem.

CD-4335 *Brain-Boosting Math*

Multiplication Boxes

A multiplication box organizes factors differently.
Follow the directions below to use this multiplication strategy.

Example:

- Write the first factor across the top of the box and the second one along the right side.
- Draw a grid between the factors. Add a diagonal line from the top right corner to the bottom left corner of each box in the grid.
- Multiply. Write the product of the ones in the bottom right box of the grid (one digit per half box). Continue multiplying one digit by another, writing the product in the intersecting box.
- Shade each diagonal value using a different color: ones = yellow, tens = pink, and so on. When complete, add along the diagonals. Regroup to the next diagonal when needed.

$$\begin{array}{r} 52 \\ \times\ 34 \\ \hline \end{array}$$

```
      5   2
    ┌───┬───┐
  1 │ 5 │ 6 │ 3
    ├───┼───┤
  2 │ 0 │ 8 │ 4
    └───┴───┘
  1  7   6   8
```

Use multiplication boxes to solve the problems.

A. $\begin{array}{r} 92 \\ \times\ 47 \\ \hline \end{array}$

B. $\begin{array}{r} 54 \\ \times\ 26 \\ \hline \end{array}$

C. $\begin{array}{r} 61 \\ \times\ 85 \\ \hline \end{array}$

D. $\begin{array}{r} 946 \\ \times\ 23 \\ \hline \end{array}$

E. $\begin{array}{r} 719 \\ \times\ 15 \\ \hline \end{array}$

F. $\begin{array}{r} 621 \\ \times\ 87 \\ \hline \end{array}$

G. $\begin{array}{r} 489 \\ \times\ 239 \\ \hline \end{array}$

H. $\begin{array}{r} 253 \\ \times\ 746 \\ \hline \end{array}$

I. $\begin{array}{r} 169 \\ \times\ 815 \\ \hline \end{array}$

Try additional problems on your own. Use grid paper. Try factors with more digits. Check your answers using a calculator. Share your results with a partner.

Choose three problems from this page. Use the place-value drawing strategy to solve one and the breaking-apart strategies to solve the other two.

Pulling It All Together

 multiplication strategies

You now know five different strategies for solving multiplication problems: place-value drawings, breaking apart completely, breaking apart partially, multiplication boxes, and the way you were using before learning these new methods. Try all five strategies with the problems below. Do the place-value drawings on the back of this page.

A. 56 x 98

B. 76 x 239

C. 123 x 142

D. 4 x 2452

Which method works best for you? Explain your understanding of this strategy.

_____

_____

_____

Are there strategies you prefer for different problems? Explain.

_____

_____

_____

Make sure you use a strategy you understand. Getting the right answer is not enough!

CD-4335 *Brain-Boosting Math*

Basketball

two-digit x four-digit multiplication/place value

Solve.

1 3388
        x   56

2 2253
        x   45

3 7806
        x   37

4 7994
        x   79

5 3446
        x   86

6 6261
        x   61

7 2638
        x   46

8 2365
        x   12

9 1748
        x   36

10 2633
         x   48

11 4206
         x   21

12 1468
         x   99

The Odds and the Evens are playing the final game of the season. Find each team's score to discover who won the game. Scoring is as follows:

- A 1 in the thousands place is worth a one-point free throw.
- A 2 in the tens place is worth a two-point shot.
- A 3 in the hundreds place is worth a three-point shot.

It is possible to have more than one shot per answer.

Determine the score for each odd and even problem. Write the score below in the ball with the correct problem number. Add to find each team's total score.

Odds

1   3   5
7   9   11

Evens

2   4   6
8   10   12

Total scores

Odds _____

Evens _____

Who won?

_____

Delicate Operation

Solve. Using only the digits from each product in order, write a number sentence that equals the given number. Follow the order of operations.

A. 56732
    x   34

    _____ = 49

B. 3721
    x 236

    _____ = 44

C. 1642
    x 195

    _____ = 45

D. 1135
    x 714

    _____ = 27

E. 3261
    x 306

    _____ = 61

F. 963
    x 562

    _____ = 60

G. 4526
    x 718

    _____ = 6

H. 2361
    x 507

    _____ = 63

I. Using only the digits from the product on the right in order, write three number sentences to equal three different answers. Follow the order of operations.

    _____

    _____

    _____

    2429
    x 672

Compare your answers with those of two classmates. Draw an X next to any sequences that are the same. Circle the ones that are yours alone.

Pyramid

multiplication and division/problem solving

Multiply and divide your way to the top! Multiply adjacent numbers and write the product in the box above them. Use multiplication and division to fill in every box.

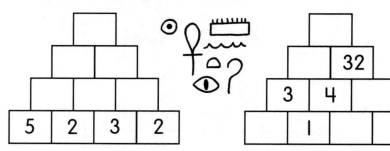

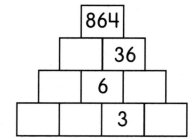

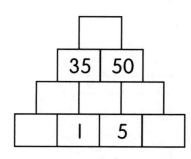

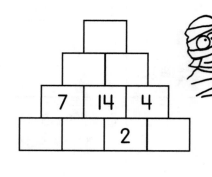

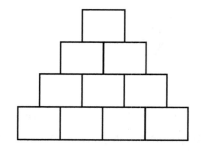

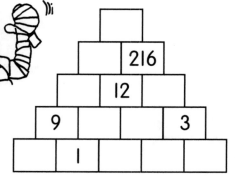

Write your own. Fill in the bottom row in each pyramid on the left. Then, multiply your way to the top. Check your answers with a calculator.

Fill in the bottom row in each pyramid on the right. Leave the rest of the boxes blank. Fold back along the fold line to hide the answers. Trade with a friend.

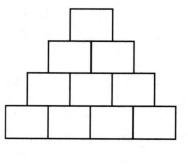

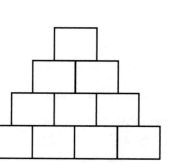

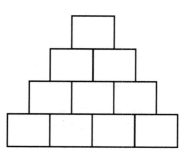

fold

CD-4335 *Brain-Boosting Math*

Multiplication Hourglass

problem solving/factors

To fill in the hourglass, multiply and divide your way from the middle box. Split the middle number into two factors. Write the factors in the two boxes below the first number. Continue until you reach the bottom row. Then, use two different factors and work your way up. The top and bottom rows of numbers in each hourglass must be different.

Example:

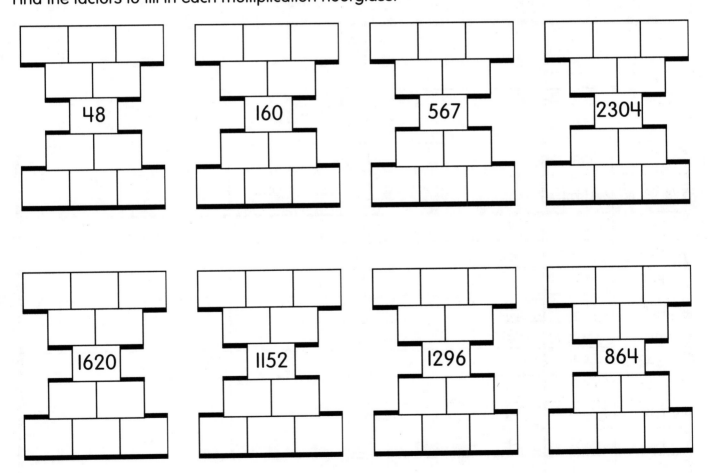

Find the factors to fill in each multiplication hourglass.

Compare hourglasses with a classmate. Draw a star next to each number you have that your classmate does not have.

 Speeding Tickets

Study the fine schedule. Fill in the chart. Use the chart to answer the questions on page 51.

Fine Schedule

1–10 mph over the speed limit: $10 each mph
11–20 mph over the speed limit: $15 each mph
>20 mph over the speed limit: $20 each mph

Example: 15 mph over the speed limit
The fine for the first 10 mph over is 10 x $10 or $100. The fine for the next 5 mph over is 5 x $15 or $75. Total fine = $175.

* Indicates speeding in a work zone. Fines are doubled.
** Indicates speeding in a school zone. Fines are tripled.

Name (initials)	Posted Speed Limit	Speed	Fine Adjustment	Miles Per Hour Over the Limit	Total Fine
GWW	35	50			
JKF	55	82			
ENP	45	63			
CGH	45	94			
MMJ	25	31	**		
SAE	40	62			
MRC	25	59			
DTP	15	34	**		
FEG	15	41	**		
DBF	55	67	*		
KLO	35	44			

CD-4335 *Brain-Boosting Math*

Speeding Tickets (continued)

Use the chart on page 50 to answer the questions.

1. Who received the greatest fine? _____

2. Who received the smallest fine? _____

3. What is the range in fines?

   _____

4. What is the average fine?

   _____

5. What is the median fine?

   _____

6. What is the greatest number of mph over the speed limit?

   _____

7. What is the least number of mph over the speed limit?

   _____

8. What is the range of mph over the speed limit?

   _____

9. What is the average number of miles over the speed limit?

   _____

10. What is the median number of miles over the speed limit?

    _____

11. Is the person with the most mph over the speed limit paying the largest fine? _____

    Explain._____

12. Is the person with the smallest number of miles over the speed limit paying the smallest fine? _____

    Explain._____

13. FEG makes $350 a week. If FEG pays $50 each week towards the fine, how long will it take to pay off the fine?

    _____

14. SAE wants to pay off the fine in four weeks. How much will be paid each week if the payments are equal?

    _____

15. CGH can pay $166 a week. How long until this fine is paid?

    _____

16. MRC wants to pay off the fine in five weeks but cannot pay more than $80 the first two weeks. Make a payment plan.

    Week 1:_____

    Week 2: _____

    Week 3: _____

    Week 4: _____

    Week 5: _____

Name _____

How Many in Each Group?

one- or two-digit divisors/division strategy

One way to solve division problems is to visualize the numbers. This strategy uses place-value drawings. Follow the steps below to try this strategy with the problem 1,202 ÷ 8.

1. Draw a representation of the dividend using these symbols:

   ■ = 1000   □ = 100 | = 10   • = one

   The number 1,202 would look like this: ■ □ □ • •

2. Break the dividend into equal groups. The divisor determines how many groups you will make. For the problem 1,202 ÷ 8, break the dividend (1,202) into 8 groups.

3. Begin with the largest pieces. If you do not have enough of the largest pieces to fit in each group, break them into smaller pieces. Repeat as needed with the other pieces.

   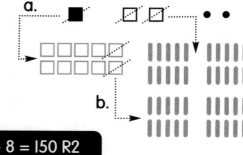

   • In the example, there is only one 1000. Break the 1000 into ten 100s. (See step a.) You now have enough to fit one 100 in each group.

   • You are left with four 100s. Break each 100 into ten 10s for a total of 40. (See step b.) You now have enough to add five 10s to each group.

   • Only two ones remain. There are not enough ones to divide evenly between groups, so this is your remainder.

4. The total value in each group is your quotient. Add together any pieces that do not fit equally into the groups to find the remainder.

   1,202 ÷ 8 = 150 R2

   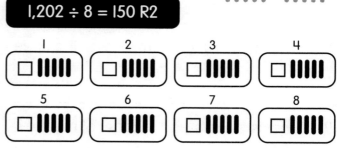

Use this strategy to solve the problems below on another sheet of paper.
Attach the paper and record your quotients here.

A. $5\overline{)3438}$ B. $31\overline{)2554}$ C. $42\overline{)6006}$ D. $17\overline{)3757}$

Explain why you can find the correct quotient using this strategy.

_____

_____

CD-4335 *Brain-Boosting Math*

Repeated Subtraction

one- or two-digit divisors/division strategy

Division is like repeated subtraction. Looking for subtractable pieces is a great division strategy. Multiply the divisor as many times as you need to get the remainder less than the divisor. Add up the multiples to find the quotient.

```
          306 R7
    13) 3985 ............ dividend
      - 1300 | 100
        2685
      - 1300 | 100
        1385
      - 1300 | 100
          85
        - 78 |   6 ...... quotient
           7 | 306
```

divisor

remainder

Example: 13)3985

Solve the problems using this strategy.

A. 7)462

B. 6)1,386

C. 5)18,089

D. 42)2,937

E. 98)9,710

F. 74)7,048

G. 28)3,330

H. 69)9,175

I. 25)71,770

J. 94)35,531

K. 46)96,819

L. 12)75,016

Explain why you can find the correct quotient using this strategy.

_____

Use the place-value drawing strategy on one problem of your choice. Use the back of this page.

CD-4335 *Brain-Boosting Math*

Elements of Math

Solve for each quotient.

C $6\overline{)54,387}$

E $5\overline{)31,078}$

A $2\overline{)95,027}$

A $3\overline{)51,026}$

L $6\overline{)57,621}$

I $7\overline{)86,572}$

S $5\overline{)90,942}$

O $9\overline{)73,418}$

G $9\overline{)52,571}$

D $7\overline{)93,628}$

U $8\overline{)71,507}$

R $8\overline{)64,056}$

Find the name of the Greek mathematician whose textbook *Elements* was the standard for nearly 2000 years. He lived from 330 to 260 B.C. Circle every answer with a remainder of 3. Write these answers on the lines below in order from smallest to largest. In each box, write the letter that corresponds to the answer.

_____

CD-4335 *Brain-Boosting Math*

Box It

Solve. Arrange your answers to fit into the grid.
Answers run vertically from left to right and horizontally from top to bottom.

A. $16\overline{)41{,}872}$	B. $63\overline{)124{,}866}$	C. $27\overline{)201{,}987}$	D. $18\overline{)135{,}288}$
E. $24\overline{)59{,}400}$	F. $32\overline{)156{,}640}$	G. $45\overline{)226{,}170}$	H. $39\overline{)266{,}760}$

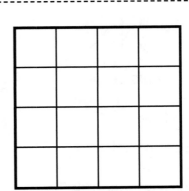

This time, work backwards. Fill in the first grid with numbers. On another sheet of paper, write eight division problems whose answers could be arranged into it. To do this, multiply each number in the grid by a two-digit number. The product becomes the dividend, and the two-digit number becomes the divisor. Fold the numbered grid back so only the empty one is showing. Give the grid and the division problems to a classmate to solve. When finished, your classmate can unfold the page to check the answers.

- ✂

fold

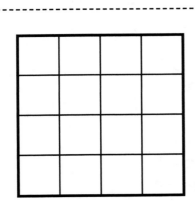

Division Venn

Solve for each quotient.

A. $40 \overline{) 72,808}$ B. $70 \overline{) 73,892}$ C. $95 \overline{) 27,148}$ D. $75 \overline{) 35,912}$

E. $81 \overline{) 49,322}$ F. $36 \overline{) 20,273}$ G. $97 \overline{) 87,215}$ H. $82 \overline{) 52,724}$

I. $98 \overline{) 42,977}$ J. $89 \overline{) 29,831}$ K. $63 \overline{) 57,220}$ L. $47 \overline{) 21,811}$

Write the quotients in the Venn diagram. Don't forget about the outside set!

Add one quotient with a remainder of your own to each section of the Venn diagram.

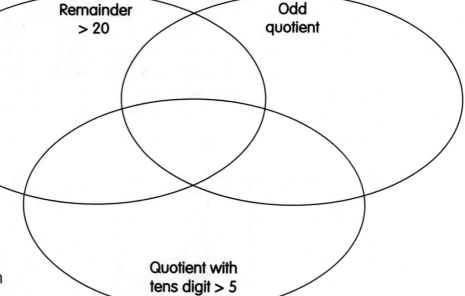

Remainder > 20

Odd quotient

Quotient with tens digit > 5

Economics Project

Christolf's class has been divided into groups to make and sell a product in order to learn about supply and demand. Christolf and his group plan to make pins out of beads.

1. They plan to make 375 pins. They have one month to make them. If the month has 30 days, how many pins should they make each day?

2. Each pin takes 28 beads. How many beads do they need?

3. Beads are sold in bags of 550. How many bags do they need to buy?

4. Each bag of beads costs $2.50. What is the total cost of the beads?

5. The pins come in packs of 30. How many packs do they need to buy?

6. Each pack costs 60¢. How much will the pins cost?

7. What is the total cost of materials?

8. The project requires groups to make at least a 30% profit. Assuming all pins are sold, what is the minimum cost they should be sold at to insure a 35% profit?

9. How much profit will they make if they sell the pins for 25¢?

   30¢?

   35¢?

Name _____

Town Toy Store is having a month-long sale. The prices on selected items drop lower every five days. Find the price at each level of the sale and fill in the table. Discounts are taken from the regular price, not the previous sale price.

Remember: To determine a price at 10% off, multiply by .10 and subtract from the original price OR multiply the original price by .90.

Popular items will go fast! | Just **LOOK** at those prices! | Get your toys while you can!

| | | Days 1–5 | Days 6–10 | Days 11–15 | Days 16–20 | Days 21–25 | Days 26–30 |
Item	Regular Price	10% off	15% off	20% off	25% off	50% off	75% off
Trading Cards	$3.75						
Game Cartridge	$38.99						
CD	$23.00						
Movie Figures	$19.99						
Soccer Ball	$26.25						

Use the table to answer the questions.

1. Is there a "Big Sale" the first 15 days? Explain.

   _____

2. When do you consider the start of the "Big Sale"? Explain.

   _____

How might the following affect your decision to make a purchase?

3. You have $12 and want to buy one of the movie figures.

   _____

4. There are only five game cartridges left and you have been saving for one for months. You have enough to buy one at full price.

   _____

5. You have $20. Your sister might like a CD for her birthday next week.

   _____

6. The soccer ball is the most popular one there is. They finally got in a shipment just for the sale.

   _____

Work Space

CD-4335 *Brain-Boosting Math*

Totem Pole

Help organize the totem pole. Write the three decimals on the lines, then add to find the sum. Write a number from 1 to 8 in each totem to put the answers in order from greatest to least.

1. nine point zero zero six
   ninety-one point two zero two
   two hundred fifty-eight point nine zero one

   _____
   _____
   + _____

    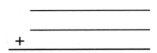

2. five hundred four point zero three
   point zero nine seven
   ninety-one point zero five six

   _____
   _____
   + _____

3. point four nine eight
   twelve point six five eight
   three hundred point nine

   _____
   _____
   + _____

4. one hundred twenty-four point zero zero three
   sixteen point one four six
   six hundred five point zero zero nine

   _____
   _____
   + _____

    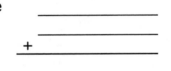

5. one point zero zero two
   three point zero zero nine
   eighty point zero six five

   _____
   _____
   + _____

    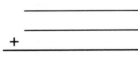

6. twenty-one point zero two three
   one point nine eight four
   seventy-eight point three

   _____
   _____
   + _____

   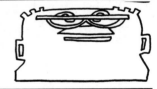 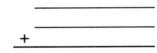

7. point eight zero four
   two hundred twenty-four point eight
   three point zero zero four

   _____
   _____
   + _____

    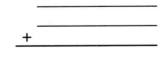

8. two hundred thirty-one point zero two
   sixty-four point eight five one
   point zero four eight

   _____
   _____
   + _____

    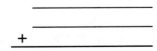

Discovering Diamonds

addition with decimals/place value

Align the addends. Find each sum. Then, read below to discover what gemstones you have.

A. 24.81
    .0516
    256.01
    34.813 + _____

B. 56.092
    1.003
    24.002
    100.034 + _____

C. 90.17
    3.781
    46.3082
    .7408 + _____

D. 596.1214
    .0029
    4.4303
    2.042 + _____

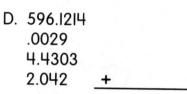

E. 5.2056
    63.521
    403.1602
    7.3433 + _____

F. 7.3024
    329.5105
    .642
    41.2205 + _____

G. 5.0501
    460.8
    2.519
    96.1448 + _____

H. 798.27
    3.5082
    16.0176
    .9236 + _____

I. 8.844
    3.641
    .0258
    13.0115 + _____

J. 50.32
    37.7528
    180.576
    .9077 + _____

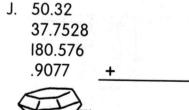

K. .0479
    3.428
    22.8041
    43.72 + _____

L. 18.052
    5.9467
    1.4089
    489.965 + _____

Use the clues to determine what gemstones you have found.
- A diamond is a whole number. Circle each diamond.
- A ruby has a 3 in the hundredths place. Color each ruby red.
- A topaz has a 2 in the thousandths place. Color each topaz yellow.
- An emerald has a 3 in the hundreds place. Color each emerald green.

CD-4335 *Brain-Boosting Math*

Just Jousting

decimals in word form/subtraction with decimals

Use the decimals to write three subtraction problems on the shields. Solve. The winner of each joust holds the shield with the largest difference. Draw a star above each winner.

1. thirty-five point eight zero six

    forty point nine zero four

    eighteen point zero nine nine

2. two point one seven five

    twenty-five point zero nine two

    sixteen point one five three

3. forty-one point five zero two

    thirty-nine point nine two four

    eighteen point eight four six

4. sixty point one five

    forty-seven point seven zero five

    forty-two point eight nine

5. two point nine seven nine

    thirty point five

    fifteen point seven six

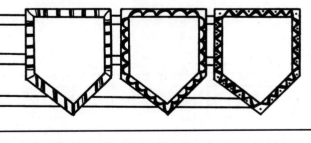

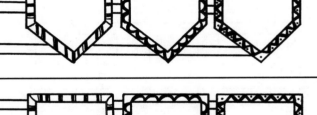

CD-4335 *Brain-Boosting Math*

Start Where You Left Off

addition and subtraction with decimals

Solve. Use the answer to start the next problem.

A. $\begin{array}{r} 45.7 \\ + 354.24 \\ \hline \end{array}$

B. $\begin{array}{r} \boxed{} \\ - 24.006 \\ \hline \end{array}$

C. $\begin{array}{r} \boxed{} \\ - 269.824 \\ \hline \end{array}$

D. $\begin{array}{r} \boxed{} \\ + 6.89 \\ \hline \end{array}$

E. $\begin{array}{r} \boxed{} \\ - 45.62 \\ \hline \end{array}$

F. $\begin{array}{r} \boxed{} \\ - 9.8 \\ \hline \end{array}$

G. $\begin{array}{r} \boxed{} \\ + 29.78 \\ \hline \end{array}$

H. $\begin{array}{r} \boxed{} \\ + 53.77 \\ \hline \end{array}$

I. $\begin{array}{r} \boxed{} \\ - 56.09 \\ \hline \end{array}$

J. $\begin{array}{r} \boxed{} \\ - 28.28 \\ \hline \end{array}$

K. $\begin{array}{r} \boxed{} \\ + 9.185 \\ \hline \end{array}$

L. $\begin{array}{r} \boxed{} \\ + 18.47 \\ \hline \end{array}$

M. $\begin{array}{r} \boxed{} \\ - 0.638 \\ \hline \end{array}$

N. $\begin{array}{r} \boxed{} \\ + 62.023 \\ \hline \end{array}$

O. $\begin{array}{r} \boxed{} \\ - 29.42 \\ \hline \end{array}$

P. $\begin{array}{r} \boxed{} \\ - 17.002 \\ \hline \end{array}$

Q. $\begin{array}{r} \boxed{} \\ + 4.73 \\ \hline \end{array}$

R. $\begin{array}{r} \boxed{} \\ - 79.46 \\ \hline \end{array}$

S. $\begin{array}{r} \boxed{} \\ + 7.602 \\ \hline \end{array}$

T. $\begin{array}{r} \boxed{} \\ + 13.45 \\ \hline \end{array}$

Does your final answer match the first addend on the page?
If not, go back and check your work.

START HERE   START HERE

CD-4335 *Brain-Boosting Math*

Decimal Diagram

Place these numbers in the Venn diagram below.

| 761.34 | 283.15 | 135.9 | 496.02 | 1823.19 | 973.12 | 1245 | 3.183 |

Solve for each product. Add your answers to the Venn diagram.

A. 72.43
x   34

B. 0.962
x   25

C. 82.19
x   12

D. 9.423
x   73

E. 511.05
x   43

F. 23.4
x   42

G. 30.07
x   18

H. 12.36
x   1.5

I. 32.81
x   0.95

J. 17.89
x   4.2

K. 28.25
x   1.3

L. 602.74
x   2.8

M. 856.42
x   0.84

Add at least one more decimal to each section of the Venn diagram. Don't forget about the outside set! Circle the numbers you added with red.

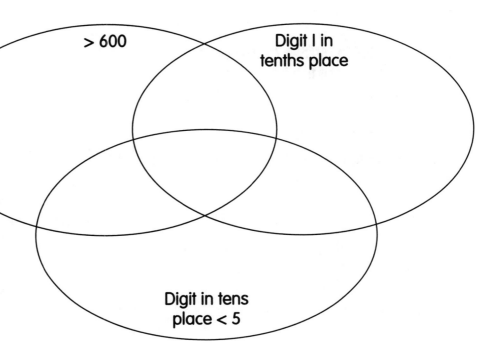

> 600

Digit 1 in tenths place

Digit in tens place < 5

Pick Those Books

addition and multiplication with decimals/algebra

Use the list of book prices to determine the price of each book in every student's book order.

1. Gerard's order totals $3.90. His two books are the same price.

2. Omarha's order totals $4.45. He ordered two books.

3. Brandon's order totals $15.85. He ordered three books.

4. Danielle's order totals $11.20. She ordered four books. Two are the same price.

5. Meg's order totals $10.85. Two of the three books she ordered are the same price.

6. Justin's order totals $21.75. He ordered five books. Four of the books are the same price.

7. Ian's order totals $5.40. He ordered three books.

8. Jon's order totals $4.85. He ordered three books. Two are the same price.

Book Prices	
$0.95	$3.95
$1.50	$5.95
$1.95	$7.95
$2.95	$9.95

9. Maddie's order totals $12.80. Three of the four books she ordered are the same price. The price of those three is less than the price of the other book.

10. Tia's order totals $27.75. Three of the five books she ordered are the same price.

11. Brett's order totals $19.60. He ordered eight books. Their prices can be grouped this way: three at one price, two at a second price, two at a third price, and one at a fourth price.

Swedish Scientist

Find the quotient.

A. $8\overline{)56.8}$ B. $4\overline{)44.8}$ C. $6\overline{)54.48}$ D. $8\overline{)496.16}$

E. $13\overline{)282.1}$ F. $21\overline{)787.5}$ G. $32\overline{)540.8}$ H. $23\overline{)646.99}$

I. $21\overline{)805.77}$ J. $14\overline{)302.4}$ K. $36\overline{)442.8}$ L. $41\overline{)438.7}$

Shade in your answers. Add up the shaded numbers on each side of the scale.
The scale tips in favor of the correct answer.

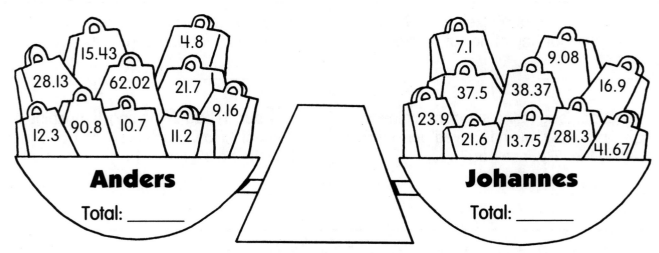

Anders

Total: _____

Johannes

Total: _____

What is the first name of the Swedish scientist
who invented the Celsius thermometer scale? _____

CD-4335 *Brain-Boosting Math*

I Only Want One

division with decimals

Round each answer to the nearest penny.

1. A 12-ounce can of pop costs 75 cents. How much for one ounce?

    _____

2. A package containing 8 hamburger buns costs $2.09. How much for one bun?

    _____

3. A package containing 13 large carrots costs 89 cents. How much for one carrot?

    _____

4. A jar containing 21 pickles costs $2.35. How much for one pickle?

    _____

5. A box of 24 cupcakes is $3.55. How much for one cupcake?

    _____

    The same cupcake in the snack machine is 50 cents. How much is saved per cupcake buying the box of 24?

    _____

6. A 12-pack of cola costs $3.75. How much for one can?

    _____

    The same can is $0.75 in the pop machine. How much is saved per can buying it in the 12 pack?

    _____

7. A 12-ounce bag of pretzels is $0.99. How much for one ounce of pretzels?

    _____

    A 3-ounce bag in the snack machine is 50 cents. How much is saved per ounce buying the 12-ounce bag?

    _____

8. A 32-ounce bag of chips is $3.99. How much for one ounce of chips?

    _____

    A 3-ounce bag in the snack machine is 75 cents. How much is saved per ounce buying the 32-ounce bag?

    _____

Try this at home: Find the individual price of 5 items in your home.

_____ _____ _____ _____ _____

CD-4335 *Brain-Boosting Math*

Fooling You with Decimals

Fill in the missing parts of the table.

Algebraic Expression	Expression in Words
	sixteen point four divided by j
	v and six point one
	two point four times s
	k divided by point zero five
	t less than point five one
	eight point four less than g
	five point zero six more than h
	y decreased by eleven point three seven
$30.03z$	
$w + 9.6$	
$q - 8.18$	
$1.02e$	
$n - 1.45$	
$14.87 + j$	
$.09 \div m$	

Solve the expressions for each value given. Use another sheet of paper to show your work.

\multicolumn{2}{c}{$.3r$}
r	Answer
1.5	
2	
.08	
4.7	
9.02	

\multicolumn{2}{c}{$2.041 + e$}
e	Answer
56.72	
7.306	
781.4	
9.95	
.679	

\multicolumn{2}{c}{$9.09 \div w$}
w	Answer
.2	
3	
.06	
1.2	
.001	

\multicolumn{2}{c}{$f - 9.903$}
f	Answer
11.04	
22.7	
64.95	
11.453	
10.861	

CD-4335 *Brain-Boosting Math*

Rounding Power

rounding/scientific notation

Round each number to the underlined digit. Rewrite your answer using scientific notation.

Example: 4,267   4,270 4.27×10^3

A. 3,156   _____

B. 6,386   _____

C. 90,249   _____

D. 9,152,530   _____

E. 52,819   _____

F. 293,066   _____

G. 7,482,518   _____

H. 335,629   _____

I. 724,398   _____

J. 1,274,289   _____

K. 692,518   _____

L. 4,746   _____

M. 82,724,853   _____

N. 8,539   _____

O. 47,183   _____

P. 2,562   _____

CD-4335 *Brain-Boosting Math*

Assessing Shapes

two-dimensional geometry

Decide if each shape described is possible. Circle **Yes** or **No**. Draw a figure for each possible shape and label with the number of the statement. Use another sheet of paper if necessary.

1.   Yes   No   a polygon that is a quadrilateral

2.   Yes   No   a trapezoid that is not a quadrilateral

3.   Yes   No   a hexagon with two right angles

4.   Yes   No   a pentagon with a perimeter of 12 cm

5.   Yes   No   a triangle with two acute angles

6.   Yes   No   an octagon that is not a trapezoid

7.   Yes   No   a trapezoid that is not a parallelogram

8.   Yes   No   a rectangle with sides 3, 4, and 5 cm

9.   Yes   No   a hexagon that is not a polygon

10.   Yes   No   a square that is not a rectangle

11.   Yes   No   an octagon with sides 3, 4, and 5 cm

12.   Yes   No   a triangle with two obtuse angles

13.   Yes   No   a square that is a parallelogram

14.   Yes   No   a polygon that is a closed figure

15.   Yes   No   a rectangle with only one right angle

16.   Yes   No   a rectangle with an area of 6 square units

17.   Yes   No   a triangle with a 2-inch side

18.   Yes   No   a trapezoid with one right angle

19.   Yes   No   a hexagon that is not a trapezoid

20.   Yes   No   a rectangle with an acute angle

21.   Yes   No   a triangle with a right angle

22.   Yes   No   an octagon that is a triangle

23.   Yes   No   a hexagon with a perimeter of 12 cm

24.   Yes   No   a rectangle that is not a square

25.   Yes   No   a rectangle that is a square

CD-4335 *Brain-Boosting Math*

Name _____

Measuring Angles

Identify each angle as right, acute, or obtuse. Name and measure each angle.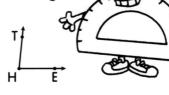

1.

_____
_____
_____

2.

_____
_____
_____

3.

_____
_____
_____

4.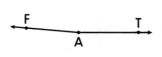

_____
_____
_____

5.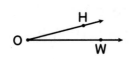

_____
_____
_____

6.

_____
_____
_____

7.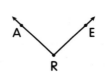

_____
_____
_____

8.

_____
_____
_____

9.

_____
_____
_____

10.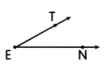

_____
_____
_____

11.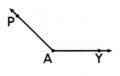

_____
_____
_____

12.

_____
_____
_____

Choose two of the above angles. Draw a figure with both angles in it. Label each vertex with a letter. Measure each additional angle and write the measurements in the figure.

Making Angles

Draw and label the following angles.

1. angle SHE, 20 degrees

2. angle WIN, 90 degrees

3. angle SIT, 120 degrees

4. angle YES, 65 degrees

5. angle ONE, 100 degrees

6. angle BIG, 240 degrees

7. angle MAN, between 45 and 90 degrees

8. angle SIR, between 90 and 135 degrees

9. angle HOT, between 100 and 150 degrees

10. angle ICE, between 5 and 30 degrees

Go back and turn each of your angles into a figure. Label each vertex with a letter. Measure the other angles and write the measurements in the figure. Name your figure. **Example:** quadrilateral MANY

Polygons

Look at the polygons. Answer the questions.

1. Name this figure.

    _____

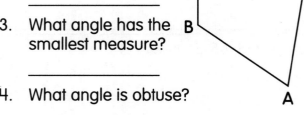

2. What angle is 90°?

    _____

3. What angle has the smallest measure?

    _____

4. What angle is obtuse?

    _____

5. Measure each side in centimeters. Label.

6. What line segment is the longest side? _____ How long is it? _____

7. What is the perimeter? _____

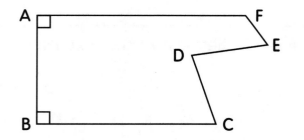

8. Name this figure. _____

9. What angle is 90°? _____

10. What angle is obtuse? _____

11. What angle has the smallest measure? _____

12. What line segment is the longest side? _____ How long is it? _____

13. Measure each side in centimeters. Label.

14. What is the perimeter? _____

15. Name this figure.

    _____

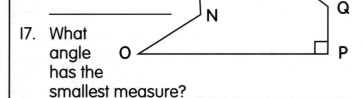

16. What angle is 90°?

    _____

17. What angle has the smallest measure? _____

18. What angle is obtuse? _____

19. Measure each side in centimeters. Label.

20. What line segment is the longest side? _____ How long is it? _____

21. What is the perimeter? _____

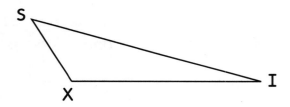

22. Name this figure. _____

23. What angle is obtuse? _____

24. What angle has the smallest measure? _____

25. Measure each side in centimeters. Label.

26. What line segment is the longest side? _____ How long is it? _____

27. What is the perimeter? _____

CD-4335 *Brain-Boosting Math*

Make the Shape

Draw the figures described. Use a pencil and a straight edge. Measure and label each angle.

1. Draw a quadrilateral with exactly one 90° angle.

   Could this quadrilateral be a rectangle? _____

   Explain. _____

2. Draw three quadrilaterals, each with at least one 90° angle. Draw one that is a rectangle but not a square. Draw one that is a rectangle and a square. Draw one that is not a rectangle.

3. Draw a triangle with one angle that is 110°.

   Could this triangle be a right triangle? _____

   Explain. _____

4. Is it possible to draw a triangle with an angle that is 180°? If yes, draw it. If no, explain why not.

   _____

5. Draw two pentagons, each with an angle that is 72°. Make one that is a regular pentagon and one that is not a regular pentagon.

6. Draw two hexagons, each with an angle that is 60°. Make one that is a regular hexagon and one that is not a regular hexagon.

7. Draw two octagons, each with an angle that is 45°. Make one that is a regular octagon and one that is not a regular octagon.

Album Areas

Make a sketch. Solve.

1. Maddie's photo album contains 12" x 12" pages. She wants to put 3" x 5" photos in it. Without cutting or overlapping, how many photos can she put on a page?

2. Maddie's new photos measure 4" x 6". How many of these can she fit on a page without cutting or overlapping?

3. Maddie likes to put as many photos on a page as possible. She has 3" x 5", 4" x 6", and 5" x 7" photos. Provide three different layout possibilities if she uses at least one of each size photo on a page. Do not cut or overlap the photos.

4. Provide another three layout options if Maddie can cut or overlap one inch from one side of any size photo. Use 3" x 5", 4" x 6", and 5" x 7" photos.

5. Maddie has a second album. This one has pages that are $8\frac{1}{2}$" x 11". Using the same size photos and the option of cutting one inch from one side of any photo, provide three layout options.

6. Maddie's third album has 12" x 15" pages. Provide three layout options for this book.

Zoo Homes

volume/surface area

The zoo is busy designing new homes for various animals. They need to  know the volume of each container and the surface area before purchasing materials. Sketch each container described. Then answer the questions.

1. 15 x 20 x 13 feet

    a. What is the volume? _____
    b. What is the surface area? _____
    c. What animal would you place in this home? Explain.

    _____
    _____

2. 12 x 8 x 24 inches

    a. What is the volume? _____
    b. What is the surface area? _____
    c. What animal would you place in this home? Explain.

    _____
    _____

3. 2 x 4 x 7 feet

    a. What is the volume? _____
    b. What is the surface area? _____
    c. What animal would you place in this home? Explain.

    _____
    _____

4. 14 x 29 x 60 centimeters

    a. What is the volume? _____
    b. What is the surface area? _____
    c. What animal would you place in this home? Explain.

    _____
    _____

5. 12 x 12 x 26 meters

    a. What is the volume? _____
    b. What is the surface area? _____
    c. What animal would you place in this home? Explain.

    _____
    _____

CD-4335 *Brain-Boosting Math*

Storage Containers

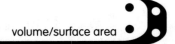

volume/surface area

Design a container with rectangular sides to hold each given volume. Sketch your container. Provide the dimensions and the surface area of your container.

1. 512 cubic units
   Dimensions: _____
   Surface area: _____

   _____

2. 729 cubic units
   Dimensions: _____
   Surface area: _____

   _____

3. 600 cubic units
   Dimensions: _____
   Surface area: _____

   _____

4. 360 cubic units _____
   Dimensions: _____
   Surface area: _____

   _____

5. 240 cubic units
   Dimensions: _____
   Surface area: _____

   _____

6. 216 cubic units
   Dimensions: _____
   Surface area: _____

Compare your designs to a classmates' designs. Check for accuracy first. Whose container used the most surface area? Why would surface area be a consideration when constructing these containers?

_____

_____

CD-4335 *Brain-Boosting Math*

Name _____

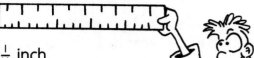

Follow the directions.

1. Measure each line using inches. Round to the nearest $\frac{1}{16}$ inch.

━━━━━━━━━━ _____   _____

━━━━━━━━━━━━━━━━━━━━━━━━━━━━━━━━

2. What is the difference in length between the two lines? _____

3. Find two items between these two lengths. List them below. Measure and write each length in inches to the nearest $\frac{1}{16}$ inch. Have a partner check your work and initial each line.

   _____

   _____

4. Measure each line using centimeters. Round to the nearest millimeter.

━━━━━━━━━━ _____   _____

━━━━━━━━━━━━━━━━━━━━━━━━━━━━━━━━

5. What is the difference in length between the two lines? _____

6. Find two items between these two lengths. List them below. Measure and write each length in centimeters to the nearest millimeter. Have a partner check your work and initial each line.

   _____

   _____

7. What units would you use to measure each length? Underline according to the key:

   | inches or centimeters = red | feet or meters = yellow | miles or kilometers = green |

   a. length of lunchroom
   b. height of skyscraper
   c. thickness of encyclopedia
   d. distance around equator
   e. height of Ferris wheel
   f. dimensions of school photo

   g. depth of fish tank
   h. distance from New York to Chicago
   i. distance from Canada to Australia
   j. length of arm
   k. circumference of tennis ball
   l. thickness of sub sandwich

8. Choose five of the above objects.
   List their letters in order from shortest to longest. _____

Measure This

Find the area and perimeter of each polygon. Find the diameter, radius, and circumference of each circle. Measure using centimeters. Round the area and circumference of circles to the nearest centimeter. Label your answers.

Remember

area of a parallelogram = length of base x height
area of a triangle = $\frac{1}{2}$ (base x height)

circumference of a circle = 3.14 x diameter
area of a circle = 3.14 x radius squared

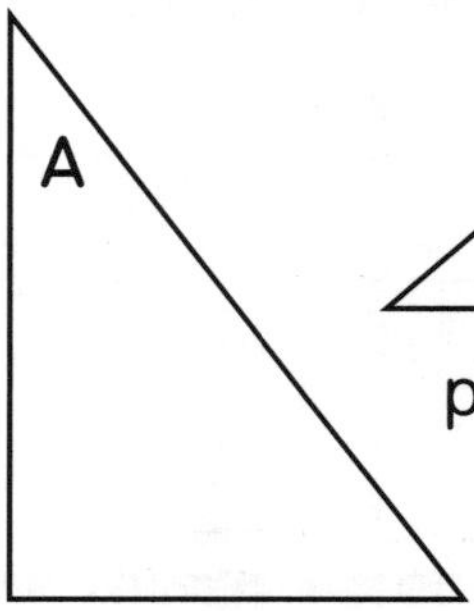

A

perimeter = _____
area = _____

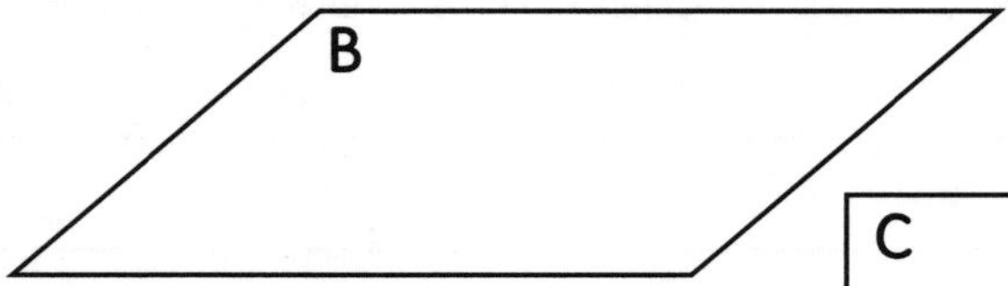

B

perimeter = _____
area = _____

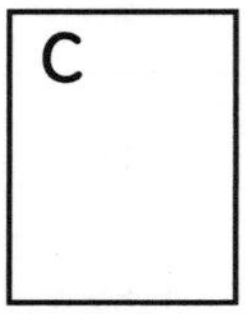

C

perimeter = _____
area = _____

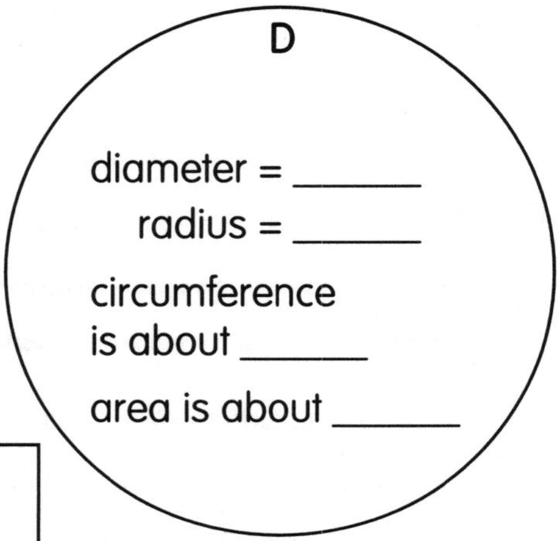

D

diameter = _____
radius = _____
circumference is about _____
area is about _____

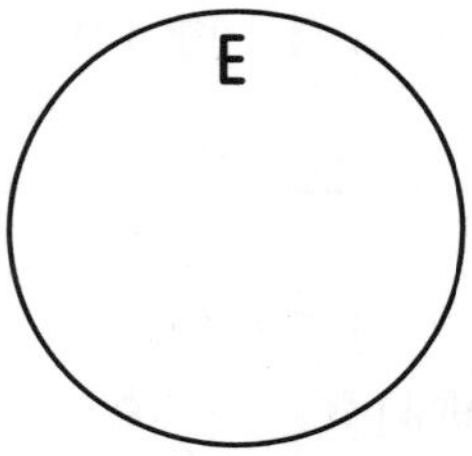

E

diameter = _____
radius = _____
circumference is about _____
area is about _____

F

perimeter = _____
area = _____

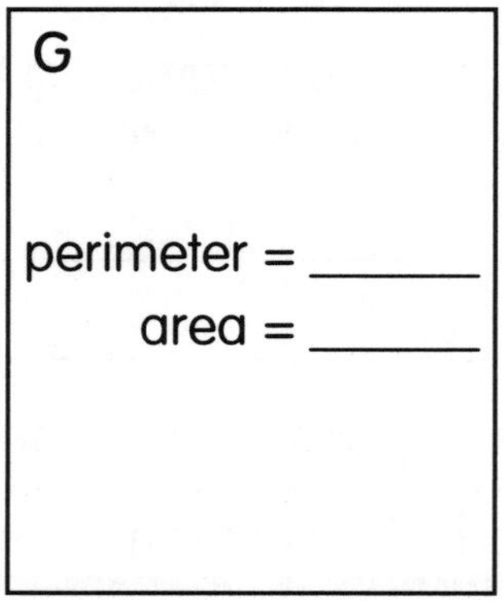

G

perimeter = _____
area = _____

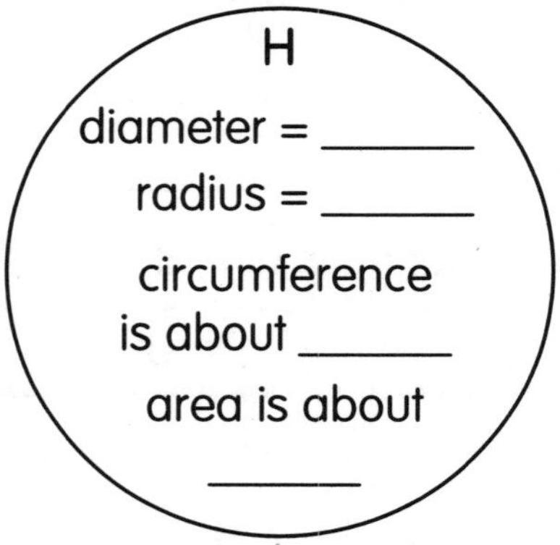

H

diameter = _____
radius = _____
circumference is about _____
area is about _____

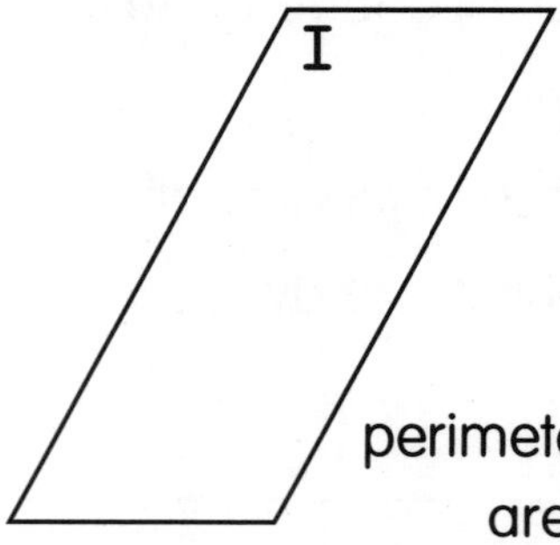

I

perimeter = _____
area = _____

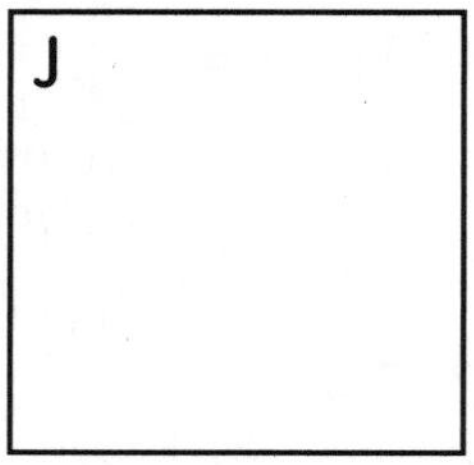

J

perimeter = _____
area = _____

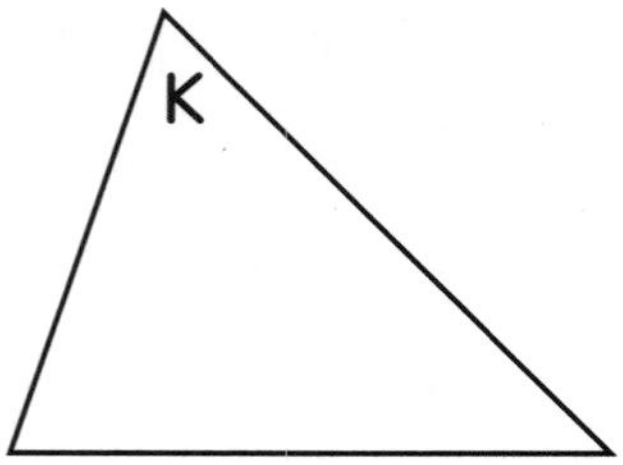

K

perimeter = _____
area = _____

Measure This (continued)

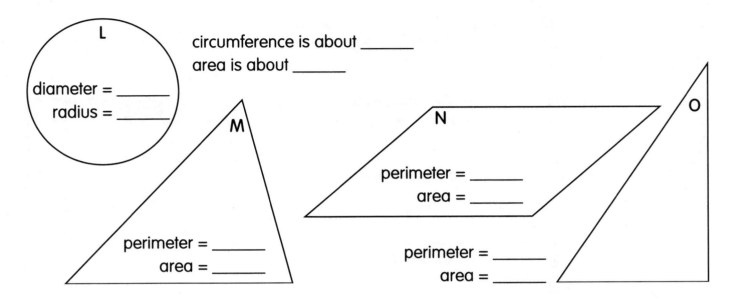

L

diameter = _____
radius = _____

circumference is about _____
area is about _____

M

perimeter = _____
area = _____

N

perimeter = _____
area = _____

O

perimeter = _____
area = _____

Find the area and perimeter of each figure below. Then, answer the questions.
_____

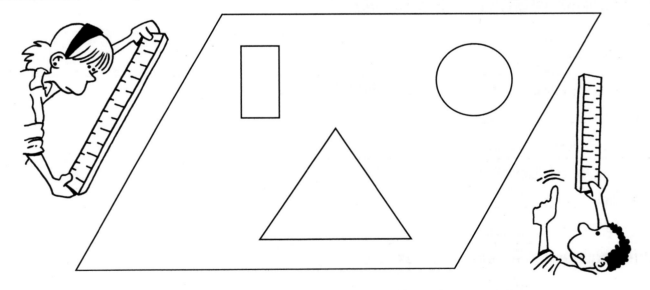

1. What is the area of the non-rectangular parallelogram
   minus the areas of all the figures inside?_____

2. What is the area of the non-rectangular parallelogram
   minus the area of the circle? _____ the triangle? _____ the rectangle? _____

3. What is the area of the circle plus the triangle?_____

4. What is the area of the circle plus the rectangle? _____

Mail It

weight/money

Use a homemade scale to weigh your mail. Set a ruler on top of a hexagonal pencil to create a balance. Use quarters for weights. Five quarters equal one ounce.

Make a sketch for each problem. Determine the weight and amount of postage needed to mail the items. Answers may involve a range.

2002 U.S. Postage Rates

0–I ounce = 37¢
up to 2 ounces = 60¢
up to 3 ounces = 83¢

1. The envelope is up and the 5 quarters are down.

    Weight = _____

    Cost to mail = _____

2. The envelope weighs the same as 8 quarters.

    Weight = _____

    Cost to mail 4 envelopes = _____

3. The envelope weighs less than 6 quarters.

    Weight = _____

    Cost to mail = _____

4. The envelope weighs more than II but less than I4 quarters.

    Weight = _____

    Cost to mail = _____

5. The envelope is down with 5 quarters but up with 6 quarters.

    Weight = _____

    Cost to mail = _____

6. Three equal-sized envelopes have a total weight of I2 quarters.

    Weight of one envelope = _____

    Cost to mail each envelope = _____

7. Five envelopes weigh as much as 30 quarters. Three are one size and two are another size. The three together weigh as much as the other two envelopes.

    Weight of envelopes = _____ and _____

    Cost to mail each = _____

    Total cost = _____

CD-4335 *Brain-Boosting Math*

Navigating the Waters

Look at the map grid. Convert each measurement in fathoms to feet and then to inches. Use these measurements and the facts below to help each boat cross the section of the lake shown.

> 1 fathom = 6 feet
> 1 foot = 12 inches

- Boat A needs 20 feet of clearance.
- Boat B needs 20 inches of clearance.
  It is not safe in water more than 12 feet deep.
- Boat C needs 11 feet of clearance.

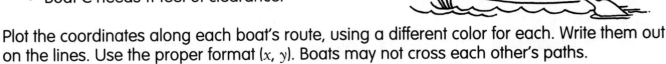

Plot the coordinates along each boat's route, using a different color for each. Write them out on the lines. Use the proper format (*x*, *y*). Boats may not cross each other's paths.

Example: Start Boat A at (0, 13), go to (1, 12), and draw a line between. Record as shown:

1. Boat A: (0, 13), (1, 12), _____

2. Boat B: _____

3. Boat C: _____

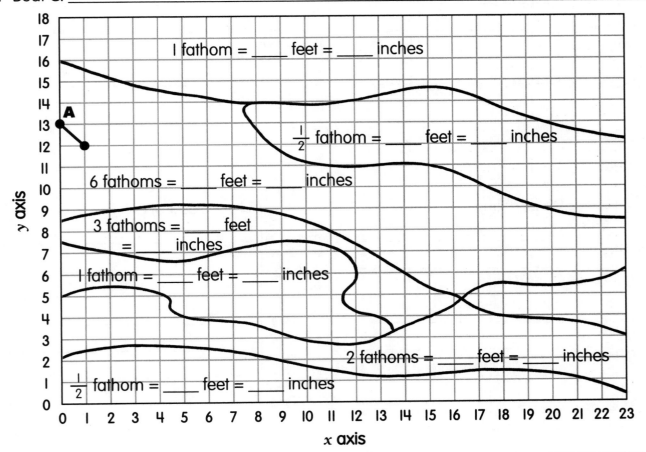

1 fathom = _____ feet = _____ inches

$\frac{1}{2}$ fathom = _____ feet = _____ inches

6 fathoms = _____ feet = _____ inches

3 fathoms = _____ feet
= _____ inches

1 fathom = _____ feet = _____ inches

2 fathoms = _____ feet = _____ inches

$\frac{1}{2}$ fathom = _____ feet = _____ inches

y axis

x axis

Temperature Tales

Celsius and Fahrenheit

Mark a different temperature on each thermometer. Each temperature should be appropriate for a different location or function, excluding the weather. **Example:** the interior of a freezer warehouse. Write each temperature in both Fahrenheit and Celsius. Describe the temperature, the location that might be kept at that temperature, and the purpose of the temperature.

1.

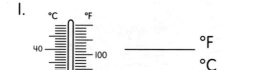

_____ °F

_____ °C

Description:

_____

_____

_____

_____

_____

_____

_____

2.

_____ °F

_____ °C

Description:

_____

_____

_____

_____

_____

_____

_____

3.

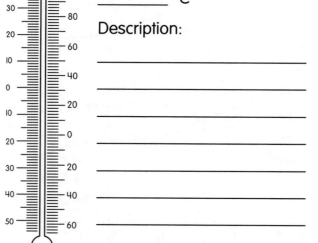

_____ °F

_____ °C

Description:

_____

_____

_____

_____

_____

_____

_____

4.

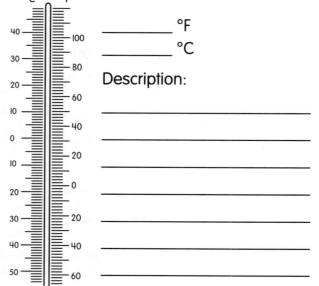

_____ °F

_____ °C

Description:

_____

_____

_____

_____

_____

_____

_____

Density Columns

Ian's class used graduated cylinders for a density experiment. Look at each graduated cylinder. Determine the increments. Mark the level of each liquid. Answer the questions.

1. Increments: _____ milliliters

    Draw the water level at 280 ml. Oil level at 390 ml.

    How many ml of oil in the cylinder? _____

2. Increments: _____ milliliters

    Draw the corn syrup level at 32 ml. Water level at 38 ml. Oil level at 46 ml.

    How many ml of water? _____   oil? _____

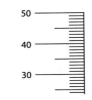

3. Increments: _____ milliliters

    Draw the corn syrup level at 122 ml. Water level at 130 ml. Oil at 134 ml.

    How many ml of water? _____   oil? _____   corn syrup? _____

4. Increments: _____ milliliters

    Draw the corn syrup level at 45 ml. Water level at 75 ml. Oil level at 90 ml.

    How many ml of corn syrup? _____   oil? _____   water? _____

5. Increments: _____ milliliters

    Draw the corn syrup level at 440 ml. Water level at 940 ml. Oil level at 1220 ml.

    How many ml of oil? _____   corn syrup? _____   water? _____

6. Increments: _____ milliliters

    Draw the corn syrup level at 50 ml. Water level at 150 ml. Oil level at 200 ml.

    How many ml of oil? _____   water? _____   corn syrup? _____

7. Increments: _____ milliliters

    Draw the corn syrup level at 7 ml. Water level at 11 ml. Oil level at 18 ml.

    How many ml of oil? _____   water? _____   corn syrup? _____

CD-4335 *Brain-Boosting Math*

Draw the Fractions

Follow the directions to draw the fractional parts.

1. Draw a group of stars. One half is yellow. One third is green. The rest are orange.

2. Draw a set of squares. Two sevenths are red. One half is yellow. Three fourteenths are blue.

3. Draw a set of moons. Two thirds are white. One fourth is yellow.

4. Draw a group of circles. One eighth is orange. Two sixths are green. Two fourths are blue.

5. Draw some quadrilaterals. One fifth is blue. One half is yellow.

6. Draw a group of triangles. Three ninths are red. Two sixths are black. One third is yellow.

7. Draw a group of ovals. Color them. Describe the colored parts using fractions.

8. Draw a group of rectangles. Color them with three colors so that fractions with different denominators can be written.

 **Draw This**

problem solving/fractions/percents/money

Draw each group of coins described. Then, find the value of the coins.

1. Two fifths of the coins are dimes. Half of the coins are pennies.
   The rest are nickels.

   What is the total value of the coins? _____

2. One fourth of the coins are quarters. One third are nickels.
   One sixth of the coins are dimes. The rest are pennies.

   What is the total value of the coins? _____

3. There are fewer than 45 coins. Fifty percent of the coins are pennies. Twenty-five percent
   are nickels. Ten percent are half-dollars. The rest of the coins are dimes.

   What is the total value of the coins? _____

4. Twenty percent of the coins are nickels. Fifty percent of the coins are quarters.
   Twenty-five percent of the coins are dimes. The rest of the coins are pennies.

   What is the total value of the coins? _____

5. Fifty percent of the coins are pennies. Half of the remaining coins are quarters.
   The rest of the coins have an equal number of nickels, dimes, and half-dollars.

   What is the total value of the coins? _____

6. Fewer than ten percent of the coins are quarters. More than half of the coins are nickels.
   Half of the remaining coins are pennies. The rest are dimes or half-dollars. There are fewer
   half-dollars than dimes.

   What is the total value of the coins? _____

Compare your total values with a partner. Are the totals equivalent? Explain your findings.

_____

_____

Coin Fractions

Look at the set of coins on the right. Answer the questions.

1. What fraction of the coins are the following?
    Reduce fractions where appropriate.

    a. pennies _____   b. nickels _____   c. dimes _____

    d. quarters _____   e. half-dollars _____

2. Which $\frac{1}{2}$ of the coins equal each amount? List the coins.

    a. $2.32 _____

    b. $2.60 _____

    c. $0.92 _____

3. Which $\frac{3}{4}$ of the coins equal $2.92? List the coins.

    _____

4. Which $\frac{1}{6}$ of the coins equal $0.80? List the coins.

    _____

5. Choose $\frac{1}{4}$ ($\frac{6}{24}$) of the coins. List the coins. _____

    _____

    What is their value? _____

6. Choose $\frac{1}{3}$ ($\frac{8}{24}$) of the coins. List the coins. _____

    _____

    What is their value? _____

You Do It:

Draw or stamp 12 coins on the front of a card. Choose a fractional part of the coins. Determine the value. Write the fraction and value on the front. On the back, draw or stamp the correct answer. Trade with a partner.

Example: front of card

$\frac{1}{2}$ = 41¢

Example: back of card

10¢ – 20¢ – 30¢ – 35¢ – 40¢ – 41¢

Fraction Riddles

Determine the answers to the riddles. Label your answers.

1. There are 8 blocks in $\frac{4}{7}$ of a set. How many blocks in the whole set?

2. There are 14 crackers in $\frac{2}{7}$ of the box. How many crackers in the box?

3. There are 5 stars on $\frac{1}{5}$ of a sticker sheet. How many stars on the whole sheet?

4. There are 34 pretzels in $\frac{2}{9}$ of a bag. How many pretzels in the bag?

5. There are 4 cupcakes in $\frac{1}{3}$ of the box. How many cupcakes in the whole box?

6. Twenty-four blue crayons equal $\frac{2}{11}$ of the leftover box. How many crayons in all?

7. There are 44 calories in $\frac{2}{6}$ of a can of pop. How many calories in the whole can?

8. Nine dimes equal $\frac{3}{8}$ of the coins in my pocket. How many coins in my pocket?

Write a riddle for each set.

A. _____

_____

_____

_____

B. _____

_____

_____

_____

C. _____

_____

_____

_____

Name _____

Gone Fishing

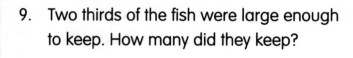

Read. Solve the problems.

1. Ian and his dad went fishing. They took 81 sand fleas along as bait. When they returned home $\frac{1}{9}$ were left. How many sand fleas did they use?

2. It took 20 minutes to dig the sand fleas. They got $\frac{7}{9}$ in the last 8 minutes. How many in the first 12 minutes?

3. They had hits on $\frac{6}{9}$ of the sand fleas used. How many hits?

4. They reeled in fish on $\frac{4}{6}$ of the hits. How many fish were reeled in?

5. Of the fish caught, $\frac{5}{9}$ were whiting. How many whiting did they catch?

6. Of the fish caught, $\frac{1}{6}$ were pompano. How many pompano did they catch?

7. Of the fish caught, $\frac{1}{4}$ were sheepshead. How many sheepshead were caught?

8. The rest of the fish were sea bass. How many sea bass were caught?

9. Two thirds of the fish were large enough to keep. How many did they keep?

    How many did they throw back?

10. For dinner that evening, the family ate $\frac{1}{2}$ of the fish that were kept. How many did they have for dinner?

11. Meg ate $\frac{1}{6}$ of the fish. How many did she eat?

12. Ian had $\frac{1}{3}$ of the fish. How many did he eat?

13. Ian ate half deep-fried and half fried in butter with lemon. How many deep-fried?

    How many fried in butter with lemon?

14. Maddie had $\frac{1}{12}$ of the fish. How many did she eat?

15. Mom and Dad shared the rest. How many did they eat?

CD-4335 *Brain-Boosting Math*

What Time?

Answer the questions.

1. The test started at 2:20. The time limit is $\frac{3}{4}$ of an hour.
   What time will it stop? _____

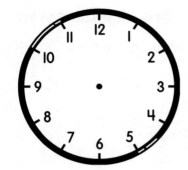

2. It is 4:35. The movie started $1\frac{1}{4}$ hours ago.
   What time did it start? _____

3. Theo has been in the pool for $\frac{2}{3}$ of an hour. It is 1:10. What time did he get in? _____

4. Willie has been playing a video game for $1\frac{1}{6}$ hours. It is 5:30.
   What time did he start? _____

5. Ona got on her bike at 4:15. It takes $\frac{5}{6}$ of an hour to get to piano lessons.
   What time will she get there? _____

6. Mom ordered dinner from a restaurant at 5:50. It will be ready in $\frac{2}{3}$ of an hour.
   What time will it be ready for pick up? _____

7. Kyle wants to read for $\frac{3}{5}$ of an hour. He starts at 2:25. What time will he stop? _____

8. The song set lasted $\frac{3}{10}$ of an hour. It ended at 4:00. What time did it start? _____

9. The bus will arrive in $\frac{1}{20}$ of an hour. It is 8:25. What time will the bus arrive? _____

10. Ian has been in the dentist's chair for $\frac{6}{10}$ of an hour. It is 4:20.
    What time did he sit down? _____

CD-4335 *Brain-Boosting Math*

Tic-Tac-Toe Fractions

Write each fraction in lowest terms.

Draw an X on these reduced fractions in the grids.

A. $\frac{6}{9}$ =

B. $\frac{3}{18}$ =

C. $\frac{5}{20}$ =

D. $\frac{24}{30}$ =

E. $\frac{14}{16}$ =

F. $\frac{24}{48}$ =

G. $\frac{28}{63}$ =

H. $\frac{21}{33}$ =

I. $\frac{15}{21}$ =

J. $\frac{18}{48}$ =

K. $\frac{4}{36}$ =

L. $\frac{5}{40}$ =

M. $\frac{8}{28}$ =

$\frac{2}{3}$	$\frac{2}{5}$	$\frac{3}{5}$
$\frac{1}{3}$	$\frac{1}{6}$	$\frac{1}{4}$
$\frac{7}{11}$	$\frac{4}{7}$	$\frac{1}{9}$

Draw an O on these reduced fractions in the grids.

N. $\frac{20}{32}$ =

O. $\frac{12}{66}$ =

P. $\frac{5}{15}$ =

Q. $\frac{12}{20}$ =

R. $\frac{35}{63}$ =

S. $\frac{12}{21}$ =

T. $\frac{8}{56}$ =

U. $\frac{30}{36}$ =

V. $\frac{36}{40}$ =

W. $\frac{14}{20}$ =

X. $\frac{6}{27}$ =

Y. $\frac{9}{45}$ =

Z. $\frac{18}{24}$ =

AA. $\frac{14}{35}$ =

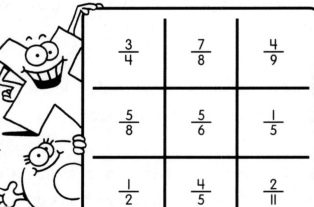

$\frac{3}{4}$	$\frac{7}{8}$	$\frac{4}{9}$
$\frac{5}{8}$	$\frac{5}{6}$	$\frac{1}{5}$
$\frac{1}{2}$	$\frac{4}{5}$	$\frac{2}{11}$

$\frac{1}{7}$	$\frac{9}{10}$	$\frac{5}{7}$
$\frac{1}{8}$	$\frac{2}{9}$	$\frac{5}{9}$
$\frac{2}{7}$	$\frac{3}{8}$	$\frac{7}{10}$

Waterfall

Look at each fraction in the grid.

- If it is less than one half, color the box red.
- If it is equal to one half, color the box yellow.
- If it is greater than one half, color the box blue.

$\frac{12}{15}$	$\frac{4}{9}$	$\frac{24}{61}$	$\frac{20}{92}$	$\frac{46}{62}$	$\frac{9}{16}$	$\frac{27}{40}$	$\frac{51}{85}$	$\frac{3}{4}$	$\frac{15}{20}$	$\frac{24}{31}$	$\frac{6}{10}$	$\frac{31}{46}$	$\frac{15}{19}$	$\frac{34}{52}$	$\frac{11}{16}$	$\frac{41}{78}$	$\frac{4}{6}$
$\frac{24}{38}$	$\frac{36}{78}$	$\frac{78}{93}$	$\frac{5}{18}$	$\frac{5}{8}$	$\frac{31}{76}$	$\frac{15}{34}$	$\frac{6}{18}$	$\frac{8}{11}$	$\frac{1}{3}$	$\frac{62}{89}$	$\frac{9}{12}$	$\frac{31}{49}$	$\frac{52}{83}$	$\frac{9}{16}$	$\frac{19}{30}$	$\frac{65}{90}$	$\frac{48}{84}$
$\frac{36}{52}$	$\frac{25}{91}$	$\frac{22}{48}$	$\frac{3}{12}$	$\frac{51}{92}$	$\frac{21}{49}$	$\frac{20}{35}$	$\frac{32}{86}$	$\frac{3}{5}$	$\frac{45}{70}$	$\frac{7}{8}$	$\frac{63}{71}$	$\frac{23}{41}$	$\frac{4}{7}$	$\frac{7}{9}$	$\frac{31}{52}$	$\frac{6}{8}$	$\frac{5}{7}$
$\frac{27}{35}$	$\frac{19}{23}$	$\frac{9}{10}$	$\frac{6}{16}$	$\frac{73}{92}$	$\frac{7}{50}$	$\frac{4}{13}$	$\frac{11}{24}$	$\frac{58}{61}$	$\frac{12}{28}$	$\frac{24}{38}$	$\frac{25}{40}$	$\frac{8}{13}$	$\frac{11}{15}$	$\frac{46}{62}$	$\frac{9}{17}$	$\frac{36}{46}$	$\frac{57}{86}$
$\frac{23}{28}$	$\frac{4}{10}$	$\frac{30}{62}$	$\frac{39}{87}$	$\frac{7}{9}$	$\frac{9}{10}$	$\frac{63}{99}$	$\frac{45}{58}$	$\frac{3}{5}$	$\frac{3}{10}$	$\frac{50}{80}$	$\frac{1}{4}$	$\frac{26}{55}$	$\frac{46}{99}$	$\frac{27}{49}$	$\frac{64}{78}$	$\frac{53}{68}$	$\frac{2}{3}$
$\frac{42}{71}$	$\frac{6}{7}$	$\frac{5}{10}$	$\frac{64}{71}$	$\frac{13}{18}$	$\frac{34}{41}$	$\frac{41}{77}$	$\frac{21}{35}$	$\frac{12}{21}$	$\frac{23}{50}$	$\frac{6}{11}$	$\frac{8}{19}$	$\frac{46}{71}$	$\frac{12}{26}$	$\frac{7}{8}$	$\frac{7}{78}$	$\frac{4}{18}$	$\frac{1}{5}$
$\frac{34}{58}$	$\frac{11}{12}$	$\frac{23}{46}$	$\frac{26}{42}$	$\frac{14}{89}$	$\frac{71}{51}$	$\frac{28}{61}$	$\frac{45}{15}$	$\frac{12}{15}$	$\frac{15}{17}$	$\frac{3}{5}$	$\frac{14}{75}$	$\frac{38}{56}$	$\frac{19}{46}$	$\frac{55}{60}$	$\frac{6}{14}$	$\frac{3}{4}$	$\frac{23}{62}$
$\frac{39}{78}$	$\frac{46}{92}$	$\frac{9}{18}$	$\frac{7}{9}$	$\frac{39}{56}$	$\frac{47}{62}$	$\frac{13}{18}$	$\frac{5}{6}$	$\frac{9}{12}$	$\frac{83}{89}$	$\frac{15}{18}$	$\frac{49}{78}$	$\frac{9}{13}$	$\frac{4}{7}$	$\frac{76}{93}$	$\frac{26}{54}$	$\frac{2}{7}$	$\frac{3}{7}$
$\frac{14}{28}$	$\frac{57}{82}$	$\frac{1}{2}$	$\frac{4}{6}$	$\frac{2}{4}$	$\frac{13}{26}$	$\frac{24}{48}$	$\frac{6}{11}$	$\frac{73}{89}$	$\frac{64}{77}$	$\frac{14}{23}$	$\frac{45}{63}$	$\frac{6}{7}$	$\frac{16}{19}$	$\frac{89}{93}$	$\frac{9}{14}$	$\frac{46}{94}$	$\frac{28}{86}$
$\frac{20}{40}$	$\frac{43}{86}$	$\frac{17}{34}$	$\frac{5}{8}$	$\frac{3}{6}$	$\frac{64}{88}$	$\frac{26}{52}$	$\frac{10}{11}$	$\frac{21}{30}$	$\frac{8}{11}$	$\frac{14}{18}$	$\frac{16}{21}$	$\frac{19}{34}$	$\frac{30}{55}$	$\frac{35}{61}$	$\frac{1}{6}$	$\frac{23}{47}$	$\frac{41}{93}$
$\frac{13}{12}$	$\frac{36}{50}$	$\frac{15}{29}$	$\frac{16}{24}$	$\frac{18}{36}$	$\frac{10}{20}$	$\frac{41}{82}$	$\frac{5}{7}$	$\frac{38}{76}$	$\frac{20}{35}$	$\frac{11}{22}$	$\frac{56}{87}$	$\frac{16}{32}$	$\frac{34}{56}$	$\frac{8}{9}$	$\frac{7}{11}$	$\frac{21}{34}$	$\frac{8}{15}$
$\frac{39}{58}$	$\frac{13}{17}$	$\frac{6}{9}$	$\frac{66}{82}$	$\frac{9}{15}$	$\frac{45}{62}$	$\frac{21}{37}$	$\frac{11}{15}$	$\frac{6}{12}$	$\frac{45}{60}$	$\frac{31}{62}$	$\frac{56}{89}$	$\frac{27}{54}$	$\frac{18}{26}$	$\frac{7}{14}$	$\frac{4}{8}$	$\frac{25}{50}$	$\frac{43}{66}$
$\frac{44}{78}$	$\frac{33}{65}$	$\frac{61}{77}$	$\frac{8}{15}$	$\frac{27}{52}$	$\frac{50}{95}$	$\frac{15}{22}$	$\frac{62}{120}$	$\frac{50}{100}$	$\frac{45}{90}$	$\frac{21}{42}$	$\frac{44}{88}$	$\frac{19}{38}$	$\frac{11}{14}$	$\frac{22}{44}$	$\frac{10}{13}$	$\frac{12}{24}$	$\frac{64}{82}$
$\frac{81}{99}$	$\frac{12}{15}$	$\frac{65}{89}$	$\frac{32}{46}$	$\frac{56}{92}$	$\frac{10}{13}$	$\frac{53}{76}$	$\frac{25}{38}$	$\frac{41}{57}$	$\frac{5}{7}$	$\frac{4}{5}$	$\frac{10}{15}$	$\frac{32}{54}$	$\frac{12}{14}$	$\frac{15}{30}$	$\frac{4}{7}$	$\frac{8}{16}$	$\frac{3}{5}$

CD-4335 *Brain-Boosting Math*

Letter Math

fraction addition with multiple addends

Use the table to find the value of each letter.
Then, add to determine the value of each word.

Example:

$$car = \frac{1}{4} + \frac{1}{2} + \frac{2}{3} = \frac{17}{12} \text{ or } 1\frac{5}{12}$$

Value Table

$\frac{1}{2}$	$\frac{1}{3}$	$\frac{1}{4}$	$\frac{2}{3}$	$\frac{3}{4}$	$\frac{1}{6}$	$\frac{5}{6}$
a	b	c	d	e	f	g
h	i	j	k	l	m	n
o	p	q	r	s	t	u
v	w	x	y	z		

1. add

2. math

3. circle

4. square

5. equal

6. less

7. tally

8. graph

9. table

10. set

11. tens

12. sign

13. coin

14. dime

15. Find the value of this sentence: **Math is fun.**

16. Find the value of your first and last names.

17. Write a sentence. Find the total value of your sentence.

Three Stars

Solve for each unknown. Write your answer in lowest terms.

A. $\frac{1}{20} + \frac{2}{10} = h$ $h =$	**B.** $n + \frac{2}{3} = 1\frac{5}{6}$ $n =$	**C.** $\frac{3}{4} + j = 1\frac{7}{20}$ $j =$
D. $\frac{1}{4} + k = 1\frac{1}{12}$ $k =$	**E.** $a + \frac{3}{4} = 1\frac{3}{8}$ $a =$	**F.** $\frac{1}{2} + f = \frac{5}{6}$ $f =$
G. $\frac{1}{2} + g = 1\frac{1}{4}$ $g =$	**H.** $t + \frac{1}{2} = 1\frac{1}{5}$ $t =$	**I.** $\frac{2}{3} + c = 1\frac{1}{9}$ $c =$
J. $z + \frac{1}{3} = \frac{13}{21}$ $z =$	**K.** $\frac{1}{6} + w = \frac{17}{30}$ $w =$	**L.** $\frac{1}{4} + u = \frac{11}{12}$ $u =$

M. $\frac{3}{4} - \frac{5}{28} = e$ $e =$	**N.** $s + \frac{1}{3} = \frac{8}{15}$ $s =$
O. $\frac{5}{6} + p = 1\frac{17}{24}$ $p =$	**P.** $\frac{3}{20} + \frac{3}{4} = i$ $i =$
Q. $\frac{1}{2} + r = \frac{4}{5}$ $r =$	**R.** $\frac{3}{14} + \frac{1}{2} = y$ $y =$

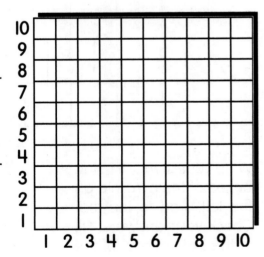

Now, use each answer to plot a star on the grid.
Use the numerator as the x coordinate and the denominator as the y coordinate: $\frac{x}{y} = (x, y)$.

Draw a star in the box where the coordinates intersect. Three stars in a row (horizontally, vertically, or diagonally) equals one point.

How many points did you earn? _____ To earn additional points, write your own problems.

Fraction Pyramid

addition and subtraction with fractions

Add your way to the top. Add adjacent numbers. Write the sum in the box above and between the two addends. Continue until you write the final sum in the top box.

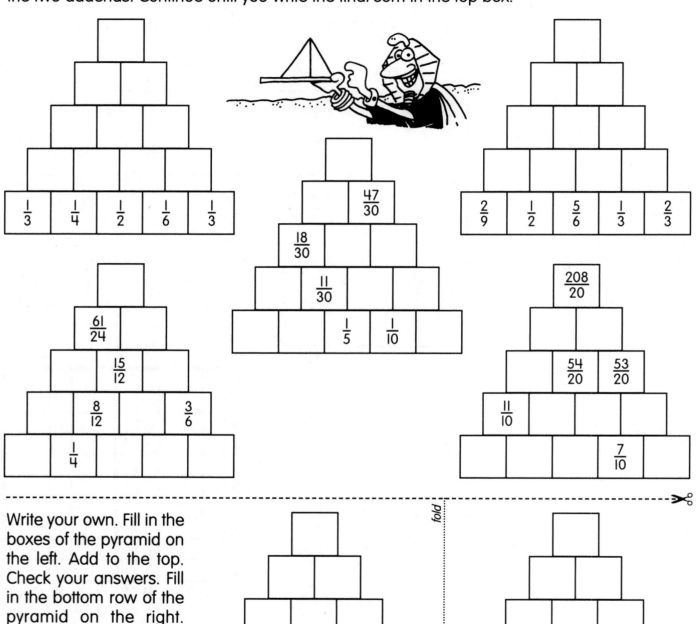

Pyramid 1 (top left) bottom row: $\frac{1}{3}$ $\frac{1}{4}$ $\frac{1}{2}$ $\frac{1}{6}$ $\frac{1}{3}$

Pyramid 2 (top middle): $\frac{47}{30}$; $\frac{18}{30}$; $\frac{11}{30}$; bottom partial: $\frac{1}{5}$ $\frac{1}{10}$

Pyramid 3 (top right) bottom row: $\frac{2}{9}$ $\frac{1}{2}$ $\frac{5}{6}$ $\frac{1}{3}$ $\frac{2}{3}$

Pyramid 4 (middle left): $\frac{61}{24}$; $\frac{15}{12}$; $\frac{8}{12}$ $\frac{3}{6}$; $\frac{1}{4}$

Pyramid 5 (middle right): $\frac{208}{20}$; $\frac{54}{20}$ $\frac{53}{20}$; $\frac{11}{10}$ $\frac{7}{10}$

Write your own. Fill in the boxes of the pyramid on the left. Add to the top. Check your answers. Fill in the bottom row of the pyramid on the right. Leave the rest of the boxes blank. Trade with a friend.

fold

CD-4335 *Brain-Boosting Math*

When Is It One?

addition with mixed fractions

Solve. Reduce your answers to lowest terms. Use the sums to answer the riddle below.
Find each sum and write the letter of the problem on the line.

E $3\frac{2}{3}$ $+\ 2\frac{2}{3}$

R $1\frac{3}{5}$ $+\ 4\frac{2}{5}$

L $4\frac{3}{5}$ $+\ 5\frac{1}{5}$

R $5\frac{2}{7}$ $+\ 3\frac{6}{7}$

M $2\frac{3}{4}$ $+\ 3\frac{3}{8}$

O $1\frac{5}{6}$ $+\ 7\frac{2}{3}$

E $3\frac{5}{8}$ $+\ 5\frac{3}{4}$

A $4\frac{1}{6}$ $+\ 1\frac{2}{3}$

T $3\frac{1}{4}$ $+\ 4\frac{3}{4}$

W $1\frac{1}{6}$ $+\ 3\frac{4}{9}$

E $4\frac{5}{6}$ $+\ 2\frac{2}{3}$

S $6\frac{1}{2}$ $+\ 4\frac{5}{8}$

O $2\frac{3}{5}$ $+\ 2\frac{6}{10}$

H $3\frac{9}{16}$ $+\ 1\frac{3}{4}$

U $1\frac{5}{6}$ $+\ 2\frac{3}{8}$

I $4\frac{2}{3}$ $+\ 1\frac{4}{7}$

N $5\frac{7}{8}$ $+\ 2\frac{3}{4}$

H $2\frac{5}{6}$ $+\ 3\frac{7}{12}$

D $4\frac{7}{10}$ $+\ 2\frac{3}{5}$

A $1\frac{1}{8}$ $+\ 5\frac{3}{4}$

Q $8\frac{4}{5}$ $+\ 3\frac{1}{2}$

T $2\frac{1}{2}$ $+\ 1\frac{3}{4}$

N $3\frac{3}{8}$ $+\ 4\frac{1}{2}$

When is it one?

$\overline{4\frac{11}{18}}$ $\overline{5\frac{5}{16}}$ $\overline{6\frac{1}{3}}$ $\overline{8\frac{5}{8}}$ $\quad$ $\overline{8}$ $\overline{6\frac{5}{12}}$ $\overline{7\frac{1}{2}}$

$\overline{7\frac{3}{10}}$ $\overline{6\frac{1}{3}}$ $\overline{7\frac{5}{8}}$ $\overline{5\frac{1}{5}}$ $\overline{6\frac{1}{8}}$ $\overline{6\frac{5}{21}}$ $\overline{7\frac{7}{8}}$ $\overline{5\frac{5}{6}}$ $\overline{4\frac{1}{4}}$ $\overline{9\frac{1}{2}}$ $\overline{9\frac{1}{7}}$

$\overline{9\frac{3}{8}}$ $\overline{12\frac{3}{10}}$ $\overline{4\frac{5}{24}}$ $\overline{6\frac{7}{8}}$ $\overline{9\frac{4}{5}}$ $\overline{11\frac{1}{8}}$ $\quad$ $\overline{4\frac{1}{4}}$ $\overline{5\frac{5}{16}}$ $\overline{6\frac{1}{3}}$

$\overline{7\frac{7}{8}}$ $\overline{4\frac{5}{24}}$ $\overline{6\frac{1}{8}}$ $\overline{9\frac{3}{8}}$ $\overline{9\frac{1}{7}}$ $\overline{6\frac{7}{8}}$ $\overline{8}$ $\overline{5\frac{1}{5}}$ $\overline{6}$

OPEN MIC NIGHT

CD-4335 *Brain-Boosting Math*

Kelp!

Help the fish find their way safely through the kelp. Safe spots are those whose denominators are multiples of five. Shade these safe spots.

$\frac{9}{10} - \frac{3}{10} = \square$	$\frac{1}{4} - \frac{1}{8} = \square$	$\frac{7}{12} - \frac{1}{3} = \square$	$\frac{1}{2} - \frac{3}{8} = \square$
$\frac{4}{5} - \frac{2}{3} = \square$	$\frac{5}{6} - \frac{1}{3} = \square$	$\frac{4}{7} - \frac{1}{14} = \square$	$\frac{2}{3} - \frac{1}{2} = \square$
$\frac{2}{5} - \frac{3}{10} = \square$	$\frac{1}{2} - \frac{3}{10} = \square$	$\frac{9}{10} - \frac{3}{5} = \square$	$\frac{7}{8} - \frac{2}{3} = \square$
$\frac{7}{9} - \frac{5}{18} = \square$	$\frac{5}{9} - \frac{1}{6} = \square$	$\frac{1}{2} - \frac{1}{5} = \square$	$\frac{1}{2} - \frac{1}{3} = \square$
$\frac{1}{2} - \frac{1}{6} = \square$	$\frac{1}{2} - \frac{2}{9} = \square$	$\frac{3}{5} - \frac{1}{3} = \square$	$\frac{7}{10} - \frac{3}{5} = \square$
$\frac{5}{8} - \frac{1}{2} = \square$	$\frac{4}{7} - \frac{1}{2} = \square$	$\frac{2}{3} - \frac{1}{4} = \square$	$\frac{7}{10} - \frac{2}{5} = \square$

Apple Picking

subtraction with mixed numbers, no regrouping

Subtract. Reduce your answer to lowest terms. Shade the correct answers in the trees to determine which tree has more ripe apples. Circle the tree with more ripe apples.

$3\frac{7}{8}$ $\quad$ $2\frac{5}{8}$ $\quad$ $7\frac{15}{16}$ $\quad$ $3\frac{1}{4}$ $\quad$ $4\frac{5}{12}$ $\quad$ $7\frac{7}{8}$ $\quad$ $5\frac{7}{9}$

$-2\frac{1}{4}$ $\quad$ $-1\frac{2}{8}$ $\quad$ $-4\frac{7}{16}$ $\quad$ $-1\frac{1}{8}$ $\quad$ $-1\frac{1}{6}$ $\quad$ $-4\frac{1}{2}$ $\quad$ $-1\frac{2}{3}$

$9\frac{4}{7}$ $\quad$ $8\frac{4}{5}$ $\quad$ $6\frac{5}{8}$ $\quad$ $1\frac{2}{3}$ $\quad$ $2\frac{3}{4}$ $\quad$ $6\frac{1}{2}$

$-3\frac{1}{2}$ $\quad$ $-2\frac{2}{3}$ $\quad$ $-2\frac{1}{6}$ $\quad$ $-1\frac{1}{5}$ $\quad$ $-1\frac{2}{5}$ $\quad$ $-1\frac{1}{3}$

$4\frac{5}{6}$ $\quad$ $8\frac{6}{8}$ $\quad$ $5\frac{2}{3}$ $\quad$ $7\frac{8}{9}$ $\quad$ $9\frac{8}{12}$ $\quad$ $3\frac{7}{10}$ $\quad$ $10\frac{5}{8}$

$-2\frac{1}{3}$ $\quad$ $-1\frac{3}{4}$ $\quad$ $-4\frac{1}{2}$ $\quad$ $-5\frac{1}{2}$ $\quad$ $-4\frac{3}{5}$ $\quad$ $-2\frac{2}{5}$ $\quad$ $-4\frac{1}{2}$

Tree A

$3\frac{3}{8}$ $4\frac{1}{8}$ $1\frac{1}{6}$ $2\frac{1}{2}$ $5\frac{1}{6}$ $3\frac{1}{2}$ $6\frac{1}{8}$ $5\frac{1}{15}$ $7\frac{1}{6}$ $6\frac{2}{15}$ $1\frac{7}{20}$ 7 $5\frac{1}{2}$ $3\frac{1}{4}$ $\frac{4}{5}$

Tree B

$4\frac{11}{24}$ $2\frac{1}{8}$ $2\frac{1}{7}$ $1\frac{3}{8}$ $\frac{7}{15}$ 9 $4\frac{1}{9}$ $1\frac{3}{10}$ $\frac{1}{10}$ $1\frac{5}{8}$ $3\frac{3}{4}$ $6\frac{1}{14}$ $2\frac{7}{18}$ $4\frac{5}{8}$

A

Choose one unripe apple from each tree. Ripen it by writing a problem here that has the fraction as its solution.

B

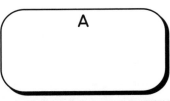

© Carson-Dellosa $\qquad$ CD-4335 *Brain-Boosting Math*

Fraction Venn

subtraction with mixed numbers with regrouping/Venn diagram

Subtract. Reduce your answer to lowest terms. Write each difference in the Venn diagram.

A. $6\frac{7}{9}$ $-3\frac{4}{9}$

B. $8\frac{1}{3}$ $-5\frac{2}{3}$

C. $7\frac{3}{4}$ $-2\frac{1}{5}$

D. $4\frac{1}{9}$ $-2\frac{8}{9}$

E. $5\frac{2}{7}$ $-3\frac{6}{7}$

F. $5\frac{1}{4}$ $-1\frac{3}{4}$

G. $9\frac{1}{6}$ $-4\frac{5}{6}$

H. $5\frac{1}{8}$ $-3\frac{3}{8}$

I. $4\frac{7}{12}$ $-2\frac{5}{12}$

J. $9\frac{1}{6}$ $-4\frac{2}{3}$

K. $4\frac{4}{9}$ $-1\frac{2}{3}$

L. $5\frac{2}{3}$ $-1\frac{14}{15}$

M. $8\frac{1}{2}$ $-3\frac{5}{8}$

N. $7\frac{1}{3}$ $-4\frac{3}{4}$

O. $4\frac{1}{5}$ $-2\frac{1}{2}$

P. $6\frac{3}{4}$ $-3\frac{4}{5}$

Q. $4\frac{1}{3}$ $-1\frac{7}{8}$

R. $5\frac{1}{10}$ $-4\frac{3}{4}$

NUMBER MIX

7 1/3 ¢

Add three mixed numbers to each section of the Venn diagram. Don't forget about the outside set! Circle the numbers you added.

Even whole number

Fractional part $< \frac{1}{2}$

Name _____

Greater, Less, or Equal

multiplication with fractions/comparing fractions

Find each product. Reduce your answer to lowest terms. Write each answer in the correct box and draw the >, <, or = symbol in the circle between the two fractions.

A. $\frac{7}{8} \times \frac{2}{3} =$ ——

B. $\frac{4}{9} \times \frac{3}{8} =$ ——

C. $\frac{2}{3} \times \frac{4}{5} =$ ——

D. $\frac{1}{4} \times \frac{4}{9} =$ ——

E. $\frac{3}{5} \times \frac{2}{9} =$ ——

F. $\frac{1}{6} \times \frac{2}{9} =$ ——

G. $\frac{4}{6} \times \frac{2}{8} =$ ——

H. $\frac{1}{3} \times \frac{3}{9} =$ ——

I. $\frac{5}{6} \times \frac{3}{4} =$ ——

J. $\frac{3}{5} \times \frac{7}{9} =$ ——

K. $\frac{3}{8} \times \frac{5}{12} =$ ——

L. $\frac{1}{4} \times \frac{2}{3} =$ ——

M. $\frac{4}{5} \times \frac{1}{2} =$ ——

N. $\frac{5}{6} \times \frac{4}{5} =$ ——

O. $\frac{4}{5} \times \frac{1}{8} =$ ——

P. $\frac{2}{7} \times \frac{3}{8} =$ ——

Q. $\frac{7}{10} \times \frac{5}{6} =$ ——

R. $\frac{2}{3} \times \frac{6}{9} =$ ——

S. $\frac{8}{11} \times \frac{11}{16} =$ ——

T. $\frac{1}{2} \times \frac{2}{5} =$ ——

A B C D E F G H I J   K L M N O P Q R S T

99

© Carson-Dellosa

CD-4335 *Brain-Boosting Math*

Five Across

Find each quotient. Reduce your answer to lowest terms. Cross out the quotient in each grid.

A. $\frac{5}{8} \div \frac{2}{6} =$ ☐   B. $\frac{3}{4} \div \frac{1}{2} =$ ☐   C. $\frac{1}{5} \div \frac{3}{10} =$ ☐   D. $\frac{1}{6} \div \frac{1}{12} =$ ☐

E. $\frac{4}{5} \div \frac{2}{3} =$ ☐   F. $\frac{2}{8} \div \frac{3}{4} =$ ☐   G. $\frac{6}{7} \div \frac{8}{12} =$ ☐   H. $\frac{1}{5} \div \frac{1}{2} =$ ☐

I. $\frac{9}{12} \div \frac{8}{10} =$ ☐   J. $\frac{3}{4} \div \frac{1}{7} =$ ☐   K. $\frac{7}{9} \div \frac{2}{6} =$ ☐   L. $\frac{4}{9} \div \frac{2}{5} =$ ☐

M. $\frac{2}{3} \div \frac{6}{9} =$ ☐   N. $\frac{5}{14} \div \frac{3}{7} =$ ☐   O. $\frac{1}{2} \div \frac{9}{10} =$ ☐   P. $\frac{3}{4} \div \frac{1}{4} =$ ☐

Q. $\frac{4}{9} \div \frac{5}{6} =$ ☐   R. $\frac{6}{7} \div \frac{1}{3} =$ ☐   S. $\frac{3}{8} \div \frac{6}{4} =$ ☐   T. $\frac{13}{15} \div \frac{1}{5} =$ ☐

Card I				
$\frac{1}{10}$	$\frac{5}{9}$	$\frac{4}{5}$	$\frac{13}{16}$	$\frac{8}{15}$
6	$5\frac{1}{4}$	$1\frac{7}{8}$	$\frac{2}{3}$	$1\frac{1}{9}$
$\frac{3}{5}$	$\frac{1}{6}$	3	$1\frac{1}{3}$	$\frac{7}{8}$
$\frac{1}{2}$	$1\frac{1}{5}$	$\frac{3}{4}$	$2\frac{1}{3}$	$\frac{7}{9}$
$\frac{5}{6}$	$1\frac{2}{7}$	$\frac{1}{4}$	$\frac{3}{8}$	5

Card 2				
$\frac{1}{2}$	$\frac{3}{5}$	$4\frac{1}{3}$	$2\frac{2}{3}$	$\frac{13}{16}$
1	$\frac{7}{9}$	$1\frac{1}{2}$	$\frac{3}{4}$	$\frac{6}{11}$
$2\frac{4}{7}$	$\frac{15}{16}$	$\frac{1}{6}$	$\frac{1}{3}$	$2\frac{1}{7}$
$6\frac{1}{3}$	4	2	$\frac{1}{9}$	$3\frac{1}{5}$
$1\frac{5}{8}$	$\frac{5}{8}$	$\frac{2}{5}$	$1\frac{1}{4}$	$2\frac{1}{10}$

The winning card must have five answers crossed out in a row, column, or diagonal.

Which card won? _____

Name _____

Fraction Hike

basic operations with fractions

Follow each hiker's path from start to finish. Perform each function along the way. Take notes by writing your answers in the empty footprints. Write the final total in the last footprint.

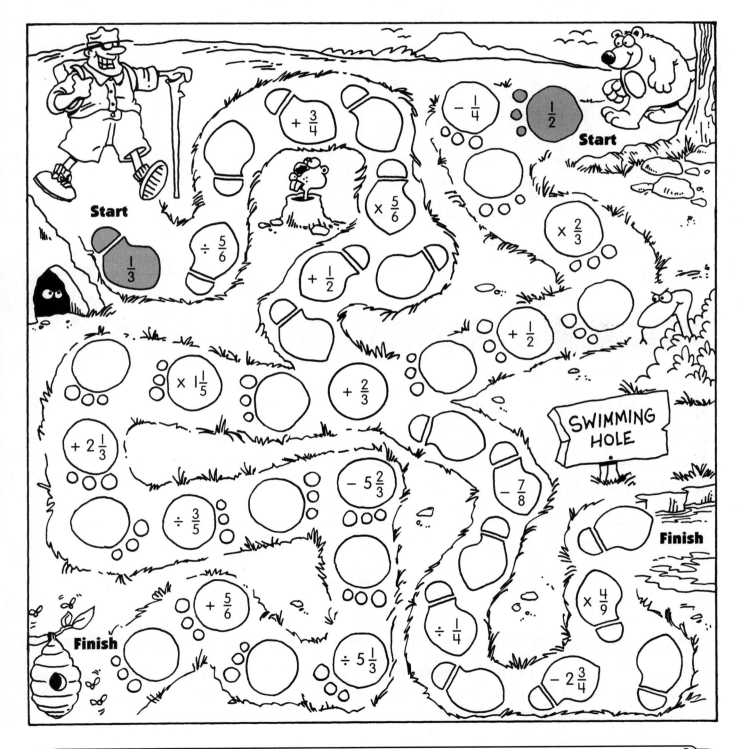

CD-4335 *Brain-Boosting Math*

Ordering Fractions

comparing fractions/basic operations

Put each set of five fractions in order from smallest to largest. Write them in the grid.

$\frac{5}{10}$ $\frac{3}{10}$ $\frac{1}{10}$ $\frac{8}{10}$ $\frac{4}{10}$

I'll have the ⅞ on toast

$\frac{1}{2}$ $\frac{1}{9}$ $\frac{1}{5}$ $\frac{1}{8}$ $\frac{1}{7}$

$\frac{2}{3}$ $\frac{1}{4}$ $\frac{5}{6}$ $\frac{5}{12}$ $\frac{7}{8}$

$\frac{5}{6}$ $\frac{4}{9}$ $\frac{1}{2}$ $\frac{1}{3}$ $\frac{1}{6}$

$\frac{4}{5}$ $\frac{3}{4}$ $\frac{7}{10}$ $\frac{3}{20}$ $\frac{2}{5}$

MENU

Use each fraction in the grid to write a number sentence. Each fraction from the grid must be the solution to a different problem. Use the given operation for each column of fractions.

Column 1: subtraction

_____ _____ _____ _____ _____

Column 2: multiplication

_____ _____ _____ _____ _____

Column 3: your choice

_____ _____ _____ _____ _____

Column 4: division

_____ _____ _____ _____ _____

Column 5: addition

_____ _____ _____ _____ _____

Compare your answers with a partner. Put a check mark next to the number sentences you both have. Circle the ones that only you have. Then, think of more number sentences. Write them on the back of this page or on another sheet of paper.

Homework Machine

functions

Apply the rule on the handle to the numbers in the top row of each machine.
Write your answers in the bottom row.

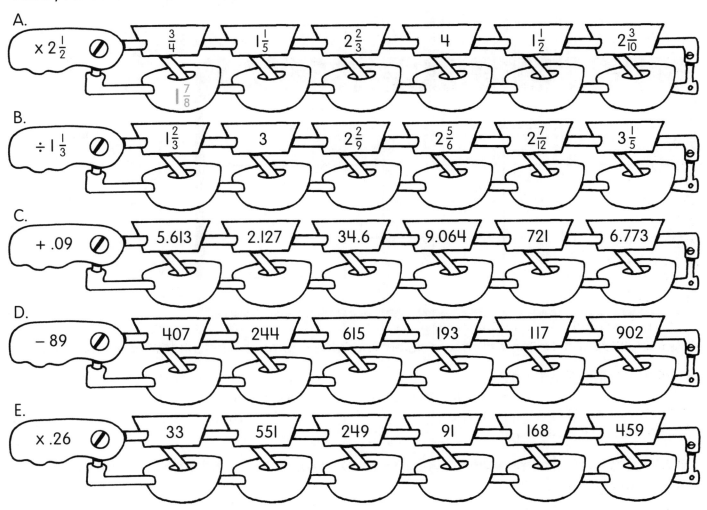

A.

$\times 2\frac{1}{2}$ | $\frac{3}{4}$ | $1\frac{1}{5}$ | $2\frac{2}{3}$ | 4 | $1\frac{1}{2}$ | $2\frac{3}{10}$

$1\frac{7}{8}$

B.

$\div 1\frac{1}{3}$ | $1\frac{2}{3}$ | 3 | $2\frac{2}{9}$ | $2\frac{5}{6}$ | $2\frac{7}{12}$ | $3\frac{1}{5}$

C.

$+.09$ | 5.613 | 2.127 | 34.6 | 9.064 | 721 | 6.773

D.

-89 | 407 | 244 | 615 | 193 | 117 | 902

E.

$\times .26$ | 33 | 551 | 249 | 91 | 168 | 459

Make your own homework machine. Decide what rule the machine will run. Write it in the handle. Write the numbers to start in the top row. Write the answers under the fold line, then fold back under to hide. Trade with a partner.

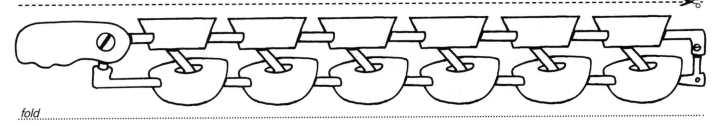

fold

CD-4335 *Brain-Boosting Math*

Number Logic

logic/number sense

Write each number in standard form next to its identifying letter in the first column of the matrix.

A. 6.452×10^4

B. $50,000 + 6,000 + 400 + 20 + 9$

C. $100,000 + 10,000 + 7,000 + 500 + 70 + 1$

D. 3.7912×10^5

E. 8.0417×10^4

F. $2.1 \times 10^5 + 600 + 30$

	Meg	Hio	Ian	Lea	Jil	Kar
A						
B						
C						
D						
E						
F						

Use the clues and the logic matrix to determine which number was chosen by each student.

- Lea's number has 0 ones.
- Kar's number has an odd ten-thousands digit.
- Jil's number has no even digits.
- Hio's number is odd.
- Meg's number has 6 digits.
- Ian's number has 2 digits that are 0.

Fill in each student's number and round it to the nearest ten thousand. Add the numbers in each list. Compare the results.

1. Meg's number is _____. To the nearest ten thousand: _____

2. Hio's number is _____. To the nearest ten thousand: _____

3. Ian's number is _____. To the nearest ten thousand: _____

4. Lea's number is _____. To the nearest ten thousand: _____

5. Jil's number is _____. To the nearest ten thousand: _____

6. Kar's number is _____. To the nearest ten thousand: _____

     + _____   + _____

     Total: _____   Total: _____

CD-4335 *Brain-Boosting Math*

Logic Blocks

Write the volume of each figure. Label your answer in cubic units.

1.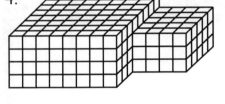

V = _____

2.

V = _____

3.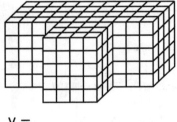

V = _____

4.

V = _____

5.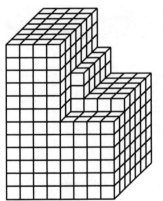

V = _____

6.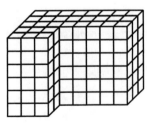

V = _____

7.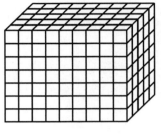

V = _____

8.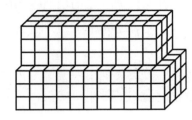

V = _____

9.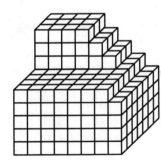

V = _____

10. How many different models can you make with 36 blocks?
    Sketch two models on the back of this page or on another sheet of paper.

Roman Logic

logic/Roman numerals

Rewrite each Roman numeral as a standard number and solve for the product. Determine each student's product by using the problem-solving matrix.

1. LVI x LVIII

2. XXXIX x XCVI

3. XLVII x LXXXII

4. LXXII x XXI

5. LXVIII x XLIX

6. XXIV x LXVII

	Wil	Ern	Dia	Nel	Bit	Ady
1						
2						
3						
4						
5						
6						

Use the clues and the matrix to determine which product was solved by each student.

- Nel's product is less than MMD.
- Dia's product is between MMMD and MMMDCCC.
- Ady's product is greater than MMMD.
- Bit's product is less than Nel's product.
- Ern's product is larger than Wil's.

Fill in the correct products.

A. Wil's product is _____.

B. Ern's product is _____.

C. Dia's product is _____.

D. Nel's product is _____.

E. Bit's product is _____.

F. Ady's product is _____.

CD-4335 *Brain-Boosting Math*

What's Next?

Look at each partial pattern. Sketch, write, or describe the next three pieces in each pattern.

1.   _____ _____ _____

2. 46, 92, 184, 368, 736, _____ , _____ , _____

3.  _____ _____ _____

4. 6, 38, 932, 1087, 12437, _____ , _____ , _____

5.    _____ _____ _____

6. zipper, yellow, x-ray, watermelon, viper, _____ , _____ , _____

7.   _____ _____ _____

8. a, in, up, the, you, cat, with, need, work, page, _____ , _____ , _____

9. Start your own pattern here. Begin with four to six pieces of the pattern. Trade with a partner. Ask your partner to add the next three pieces in the pattern.

10. Make pattern cards. Put the first four to six pieces of the pattern on the front of the card. Put the next three pieces on the back for self-checking. If the answer could vary, provide at least two examples of a possible answer.

Design a spinner for to make each set of probabilities true.
Write the numbers on each spinner.

A. The probability of spinning a 5 is 0:6.
The probability of spinning an even number is 4:6.
The probability of spinning a number < 9 is 6:6.
The probability of spinning a number > 4 is 3:6.

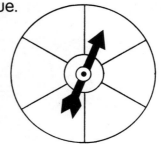

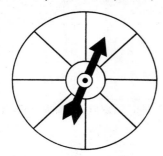

B. The probability of spinning a one-digit number is 8:8.
The probability of spinning the same number is 4:8.
The probability of spinning an odd number is 2:8.
The probability of spinning a number > 5 is 6:8.
The probability of spinning a number <7 is 6:8.

C. The probability of spinning an even number is 0:9.
The probability of spinning the same number is 1:9.
The probability of spinning a one-digit number is 4:9.
The probability of spinning a number < 50 is 9:9.
The probability of spinning a number with an even digit is 3:9.

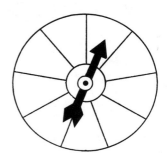

Compare your answers with a partner. Put a star next to your spinners that are unique.
Explain why your answers meet the given criteria.

Fill in the spinner. Write five probability statements that relate to your spinner.

1. _____
2. _____
3. _____
4. _____
5. _____

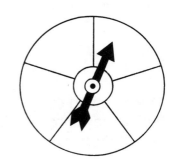

CD-4335 *Brain-Boosting Math*

Name _____

Pablo has a game that hangs bats by a magnet. He tried different combinations to determine the magnet's strength and recorded the results in the tables below. The largest bat is green and the smallest bat is red. A combination made the table if the bat added to the others already hanging caused a drop during more than two attempts.

Green Caused the Drop

Bats Hanging		
blue	red	green
5	5	3
5	5	4
4	5	4

Blue Caused the Drop

Bats Hanging		
blue	red	green
2	3	4
4	5	4
3	5	4

Red Caused the Drop

Bats Hanging		
blue	red	green
4	2	5
5	4	4
2	3	5

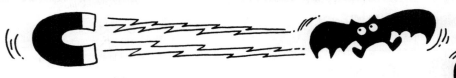

Use the data in the tables to help determine what will happen next. On each line, write: **should hang, may drop,** or **will drop**.

1. Five red, 5 blue, and 4 green bats are hanging. Hang the fifth green bat.

   _____

2. Three red and 2 green bats are hanging. Add 1 blue.

   _____

3. Two bats of each color are hanging. Add 1 red.

   _____

4. Five blue, 5 red, and 2 green are hanging. Add 1 green.

   _____

5. Five red, 3 blue, and 4 green are hanging. Add 1 blue.

   _____

6. One red, 4 blue, and 5 green are hanging. Add 1 red.

   _____

   Add another red.

   _____

7. Five red, 3 green, and 5 blue are hanging. Add 1 green.

   _____

8. Six red and 4 blue are hanging. Add 1 green.

   _____

   Explain your thinking.

   _____

CD-4335 *Brain-Boosting Math*

 **Evergreens**

Willie measured the evergreen trees on his family's property. Use the data to determine the average height of each tree type. Fill in the table. Determine increments and graph your findings.

1. Blue spruce: 34 feet, 55 feet, 42 feet, 31 feet, 58 feet
    Average height = _____

2. Fraser fir: 23 feet, 31 feet, 25 feet, 34 feet, 27 feet, 28 feet
    Average height = _____

3. Norway spruce: 55 feet, 58 feet, 49 feet
    Average height = _____

4. Red cedar: 3 feet, 4 feet, 6 feet, 3 feet, 3 feet, 4 feet, 5 feet
    Average height = _____

5. Red pine: 31 feet, 54 feet, 45 feet, 38 feet
    Average height = _____

6. White pine: 94 feet, 112 feet, 105 feet, 81 feet
    Average height = _____

Average Tree Height	
Tree	Height
blue spruce	
Fraser fir	
Norway spruce	
red cedar	
red pine	
white pine	

Average Tree Height

Average Height

Blue spruce   Fraser fir   Norway spruce   Red cedar   Red pine   White pine

Type of Tree

7. Red cedars typically grow from 30 to 60 feet tall. Explain Willie's findings.

    _____

8. On average, how much taller will these trees get? _____

9. Cross out the statements below that are not supported by the data Willie collected.

    a. Red cedars grow to be an average of 41 feet.
    b. On average, the white pines are the tallest trees in Willie's yard.
    c. The red cedars are smaller than they should be.
    d. On average, the red pines and blue spruce are about the same height.

Probability

Ratios can be written three different ways.

| 1 to 2 | $\frac{1}{2}$ | 1:2 |

Write each ratio in two other ways. Draw a picture to illustrate it.

1. The ratio of dimes to nickels is 7 to 2.

2. The ratio of bees to flowers is 9:2.

3. The ratio of spoons to bowls is $\frac{1}{1}$.

4. The ratio of nonfiction to fiction books is 4:1.

5. The ratio of fractions to whole numbers is 3 to 5.

6. The ratio of red pencils to yellow pencils is 1:5.

There are 5 red calculators, 12 blue calculators, and 4 white calculators. What is the probability of getting . . .

7. a red calculator? _____

8. a primary-colored calculator? _____

9. a white calculator? _____

The spinner below has equal-sized sections. What is the probability of getting . . .

10. the number 8? _____

11. an even number? _____

12. the number 9? _____

13. a number less than 5? _____

14. an odd number? _____

CD-4335 *Brain-Boosting Math*

Tree Diagrams

Wilson Middle School is celebrating its 50th anniversary.
Several cakes were made for the party with different kinds of frosting.

1. Make a tree diagram to show all the possible combinations.

Cake	Frosting
chocolate	caramel
vanilla	chocolate
	strawberry
	vanilla

2. How many possible combinations are there? _____

3. What is the probability of having . . .
    a. chocolate cake? _____
    b. caramel frosting? _____
    c. vanilla or chocolate cake? _____
    d. vanilla cake with strawberry frosting? _____
    e. vanilla cake with frosting other than strawberry? _____

For their final projects, Sunnie's class could choose from several topics and types of projects.

4. Make a tree diagram to show all the possible combinations.

Topic	Project
geographic terrain	map
economic influences	diorama
natural resources	report
	computer presentation

5. How many combinations are there? _____

6. What is the probability . . .
    a. Sunnie will choose to do a computer presentation? _____
    b. Ashton will choose the topic natural resources? _____
    c. Gotana will choose to make a diorama of economic influences? _____

Class Assignment

Students have been assigned to classes in the new middle school. The table shows the class assignments of the students currently in Summer's class. Use the table to answer the questions.

First Marking Period Assignments								
Science			Math		Physical Fitness		Music		
chemistry A B C			geometry	algebra	swimming	gymnastics	band	orchestra	choir
15 10 3			18	10	20	8	8	5	15

1. Summer was assigned to chemistry C. Is she likely to have her best friend from her classroom in class with her? _____

   Explain your answer. _____

2. To which math class is Summer most likely assigned?_____

   Explain your answer. _____

3. To which music class is Summer least likely assigned? _____

   Explain your answer. _____

4. Which four classes is Summer's classmate Autumn most likely taking?

   _____

   Explain your answer. _____

Fill in the last column of the table. Use the data to write the probability of each event described below. Use the ratio form ___ : ___ to write your answers.

5. Jon is a sixth-grade band member who plays flute. ___ : ___

6. Toni is a trumpet player who is in sixth grade. ___ : ___

7. Cal is a flute player who is in fifth grade. ___ : ___

8. Shalia is band member who is in sixth grade. ___ : ___

9. Anka is a fifth grader who plays the clarinet. ___ : ___

10. Chem is a percussion player who is in the band. ___ : ___

Band Instruments Played			
Instrument	Fifth Graders	Sixth Graders	Total Number of Students
flute	27	38	
clarinet	32	48	
trumpet	45	60	
percussion	14	21	
other	40	60	

Game Craze

Read each description. Answer the questions.

Ritiazul plans to enter a puzzle competition. She puts together a new 500-piece puzzle each day and times herself. Use the table to answer the questions.

Day of the Week	Time	Time in Minutes
Sunday	2 hr. 15 min.	
Monday	1 hr. 50 min.	
Tuesday	1 hr. 45 min.	
Wednesday	2 hr.	
Thursday	1 hr. 50 min.	
Friday	1 hr. 30 min.	
Saturday	1 hr. 55 min.	

1. Complete the table by converting each time into minutes. Write the times in the last column of the table.

2. Use these times to calculate the following:

   a. mean _____

   b. mode _____

   c. median _____

Izzie is playing a board game and must choose a character. He has a choice of knight and steed from those shown in the table.

3. Make a tree diagram to show all the possible character combinations.

Knight	Steed
white knight	brown horse
black knight	black horse
green knight	white horse
red knight	yellow horse

4. What is the probability Izzie will choose the following? Write ratios as ___ : ___ .

   a. a white knight _____

   b. a red knight with a yellow horse _____

   c. a black or brown horse _____

   d. a knight that is not green _____

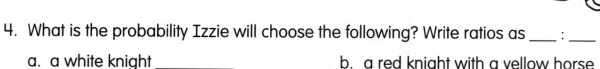

CD-4335 *Brain-Boosting Math*

For the Birds

Mikaela tallied the birds that visited her yard during a 30-minute period each day for one week.

Bird	Number of Times Seen
red-winged blackbird	II
bluebird	IIII IIII IIII IIII IIII IIII IIII
indigo bunting	IIII
robin	IIII IIII IIII IIII IIII IIII IIII IIII IIII IIII IIII IIII IIII IIII II
cardinal	IIII IIII IIII IIII IIII IIII IIII II
bluejay	IIII IIII IIII I
hummingbird	IIII IIII IIII IIII I
oriole	IIII I
chickadee	IIII IIII IIII IIII IIII IIII IIII III
finch	IIII IIII IIII IIII IIII IIII IIII IIII IIII IIII IIII IIII IIII IIII IIII IIII

Use the information from the tally chart to make a graph on another sheet of paper.
Then, use your graph to answer the questions.

1. Which bird did Mikaela see most often? _____

2. Which bird did she see least often? _____

3. What is the range between these two numbers? _____

4. What is the average number of birds she saw each day? _____

5. What is the average number of robins she saw each day? _____

6. Which birds did she not see every day?

_____

7. What evidence supports this assumption?

_____

8. Mikaela plans to observe birds a second week.
   Make two predictions based on the first week's observations.

_____

_____

CD-4335 *Brain-Boosting Math*

Raw Data

Use each set of raw data to make and interpret a graph.
Use the checklist to mark off each item as you complete it.

I. What was your favorite ride at the theme park?

Julio, Mondo Coaster
Sixto, Whip-a-Round
Erica, Gettin' Wet
Ben, Free Fall
Melina, Mondo Coaster
Jon, Mondo Coaster
Rebecca, Whip-a-Round
Omarha, Gettin' Wet
Justine, Mondo Coaster
Danielle, Mondo Coaster
Brett, Free Fall
Jacob, Free Fall
Julian, Mondo Coaster
Brandon, Gettin' Wet

Suki, Mondo Coaster
Gabe, Whip-a-Round
Justin, Mondo Coaster
Riley, Free Fall
Gerard, Whip-a-Round
Alexis, Mondo Coaster
Jesse, Mondo Coaster
Jordan, Free Fall
Didar, Whip-a-Round
Mariela, Mondo Coaster
Adrian, Gettin' Wet
Carlos, Mondo Coaster
Jena, Mondo Coaster

Checklist
☐ tally chart
☐ frequency table
☐ graph
☐ interpretation of results
  (three statements)
☐ prediction or conclusion

2. In what country were the selected 50 items made?

Singapore	U.S.A.	U.S.A.	U.S.A.	England	China
Malaysia	U.S.A.	China	England	England	U.S.A.
U.S.A.	U.S.A.	U.S.A.	China	China	U.S.A.
Canada	U.S.A.	China	Japan	Japan	China
Taiwan	U.S.A.	China	Taiwan	Japan	Japan
U.S.A.	Taiwan	China	U.S.A.	Japan	China
U.S.A.	U.S.A.	China	China	China	China
China	China	China	Taiwan	Korea	
U.S.A.	Italy	China			

Checklist
☐ tally chart
☐ frequency table
☐ graph
☐ interpretation of results
  (three statements)
☐ prediction or conclusion

Remember, you can use the category "other."

3. How fast did you run the mile?

Arturo, 12:01
Lesley, 10:57
Montes, 6:24
Tiburcio, 9:33
Sarmiento, 7:46
Paulla, 5:58
Lener, 7:02
Jesse, 9:57

Julia, 5:43
Germaine, 8:54
Rejuan, 7:20
Claudia, 11:32
Jonathan, 14:29
Jovita, 10:41
Gaspar, 8:03
Pat, 6:57

Carrie, 8:45
Aleili, 9:01
Entina, 7:56
Irma, 6:23
Sabrina, 7:59
Turrel, 8:16
Evon, 5:58
Kibili, 6:04

Checklist
☐ tally chart
☐ frequency table
☐ graph
☐ interpretation of results
  (three statements)
☐ prediction or conclusion

Try using ranges of time or rounding the times when you make the tally chart.

Use the grading sheets below to assess students' use of raw data from page 116.

Raw Data Assessment

☐ teacher copy   ☐ student copy

Student Name: _____

Title or Topic: _____   Date: _____

Are the following items included?

Y   N   tally chart
Y   N   frequency table
Y   N   graph
Y   N   interpretation of results (3 statements)
Y   N   prediction or conclusion

Do the following items contain correct information?
(If an error is repeated in another chart or graph, count it only once.)

Y   N   tally chart
Y   N   frequency table
Y   N   graph

Do the following include all parts taught, such as labels and titles?

Y   N   tally chart
Y   N   frequency table
Y   N   graph

Circle Y for yes, S for somewhat, or N for no.

Y   S   N   Is the data organized, neat, and easy to read?
Y   S   N   Do the statements about the data demonstrate understanding?
Y   S   N   Is mathematical language used correctly?
Y   S   N   Is the conclusion valid?

Raw Data Assessment

☐ teacher copy   ☐ student copy

Student Name: _____

Title or Topic: _____   Date: _____

Are the following items included?

Y   N   tally chart
Y   N   frequency table
Y   N   graph
Y   N   interpretation of results (3 statements)
Y   N   prediction or conclusion

Do the following items contain correct information?
(If an error is repeated in another chart or graph, count it only once.)

Y   N   tally chart
Y   N   frequency table
Y   N   graph

Do the following include all parts taught, such as labels and titles?

Y   N   tally chart
Y   N   frequency table
Y   N   graph

Circle Y for yes, S for somewhat, or N for no.

Y   S   N   Is the data organized, neat, and easy to read?
Y   S   N   Do the statements about the data demonstrate understanding?
Y   S   N   Is mathematical language used correctly?
Y   S   N   Is the conclusion valid?

CD-4335 *Brain-Boosting Math*

Amusement Park

On a field trip to Way Big Amusement Park, students were asked to poll 100 visitors to determine their favorite rides. They used this data to make tally charts, frequency tables, and pie graphs.

Abbie polled 100 visitors. She grouped the responses to make this frequency table.

1. Make a pie graph to display her data.

Favorite Ride	Number of Visitors
Most Popular Roller Coaster	35
Round and Round	5
Wacky Wheel	5
Very Scary Coaster	25
Underwater Ride	5
Loopy Coaster	10
Up and Down	15

2. What is the . . .

    a. range? _____   b. median? _____   c. mode? _____   d. mean? _____

3. If you were polled by Abbie, what is the probability you said your favorite ride was . . .

    a. the Underwater Ride? _____   b. the Very Scary Coaster? _____

Chambers polled another 100 visitors. He grouped the responses to make this frequency table.

4. Make a pie graph to display his data.

Favorite Ride	Number of Visitors
Most Popular Roller Coaster	25
Round and Round	5
Wacky Wheel	15
Very Scary Coaster	15
Underwater Ride	10
Loopy Coaster	25
Up and Down	5

5. What is the . . .

    a. range? _____   b. median? _____   c. mode? _____   d. mean? _____

6. If you were polled by Chambers, what is the probability you said your favorite ride was . . .

    a. the Loopy Coaster? _____   b. Round and Round? _____

CD-4335 *Brain-Boosting Math*

Amusement Park (continued)

Mikaela polled another 100 visitors. She grouped the responses to make this frequency table.

7. Make a pie graph to display her data.

Favorite Ride	Number of Visitors
Most Popular Roller Coaster	20
Round and Round	20
Wacky Wheel	10
Very Scary Coaster	35
Underwater Ride	10
Loopy Coaster	5
Up and Down	0

8. What is the . . .

a. range? _____   b. median? _____   c. mode? _____   d. mean? _____

9. If you were polled by Mikaela, what is the probability you said your favorite ride was . . .

a. the Very Scary Coaster? _____   b. Up and Down? _____

10. Whose data is most valid?

Explain your answer. _____

_____

11. Combine all three students' data into the one table below. Make a pie graph showing the information for 300 visitors.

Favorite Ride	Number of Visitors
Most Popular Roller Coaster	
Round and Round	
Wacky Wheel	
Very Scary Coaster	
Underwater Ride	
Loopy Coaster	
Up and Down	

 Gas Prices

Look at the chart of gasoline prices over a span of four weeks. Prices are listed by day.

	Sunday	Monday	Tuesday	Wednesday	Thursday	Friday	Saturday
Week 1	$1.42	$1.38	$1.35	$1.32	$1.32	$1.43	$1.47
Week 2	$1.47	$1.42	$1.38	$1.35	$1.35	$1.48	$1.48
Week 3	$1.48	$1.46	$1.42	$1.39	$1.34	$1.49	$1.51
Week 4	$1.46	$1.38	$1.34	$1.33	$1.33	$1.44	$1.44

1. What is the range in gas prices each week?

    a. Week 1 _____   b. Week 2 _____

    c. Week 3 _____   d. Week 4 _____

2. On another sheet of paper, make a line graph showing the price of gasoline per day for the first two weeks.

3. Determine the average price for each day of the week.

    a. Sunday _____   b. Monday _____

    c. Tuesday _____   d. Wednesday _____

    e. Thursday _____ f. Friday _____

    g. Saturday _____

4. On another sheet of paper, make a bar graph to show the average price for each day of the week.

5. Use the daily averages to answer the questions.

    a. Determine the price for 15 gallons on the day with the highest average and on the day with the lowest average. What is the difference in price? _____

    How much would that save over 52 weeks if you bought 15 gallons each week?

    _____

    b. What is the best day of the week to purchase gasoline?_____

    c. What days should you avoid? _____

    d. Your tank is at half on Monday. What should you do?

    _____

p. 5 — Determining Order
A. seagulls, starfish, fish, octopus, clams, dolphin
B. mammals, birds, reptiles, lunch, aquatic life, insects
C. wild blueberries, coyote, pinecones, waterfall, boulder, eagle

p. 10 — Pay Attention
Answers will vary.

p. 11 — Change a Digit
A. 8642	B. 8647	C. 8644
D. 8643	E. 6643	F. 6543
G. 4543	H. 4573	I. 4576
J. 3576	K. 3579	

p. 12 — Numbers in the Box
1. a. 42.15 b. 91.17 c. 4.43
   d. 42.15 e. 389.1 f. 389.1
   g. 91.17 h. 827.20
2. a. .85 b. .9 c. .41
   d. .83 e. .8 f. .57
3. a. 42.15, 2.59, 4.43
   b. 42.15, 389.1, 2.59, 91.17
   c. 389.1, 91.17
4. a. 2.59, 4.43, 42.15, 91.17, 389.1, 827.20
   b. 827.20, 389.1, 91.17, 42.15, 4.43, 2.59
5–6. Answers will vary.
7. 1,356.64

p. 13 — Higher or Lower?
Play the game Higher or Lower. Use the clues to find the number.

Example:
My number is between 2,600 and 8,900.
You are told that the number is greater than 2,600 but less than 8,900. Find the average of the guess and circle the guess that is closest to it. Circle 5,750 as the best guess.

Their average is __5750__
Guess: 3,000 (5,750) 8,000
Clue: lower

Now you know that the answer is lower than 5,750. You also know that it is higher than 2,600. Write the range and find the average. Continue the game.

A. It is between __2,600__ and __5,750__
   Their average is __4,175__
   Guess: 2,800 3,000 (4,175)
   Clue: lower

B. It is between __4,175__ and __5,750__
   Their average is __4,962.5__
   Guess (4,960) 5,500 5,700
   Clue: lower

C. It is between __4,175__ and __4,960__
   Their average is __4,567.5__
   Guess: 4,200 4,400 (4,570)
   Clue: lower

D. It is between __4,175__ and __4,570__
   Their average is __4,372.5__
   Guess (4,370) 4,450 4,500
   Clue: lower

E. It is between __4,175__ and __4,370__
   Their average is __4,272.5__
   Guess (4,270) 4,100 4,350
   Clue: lower

F. It is between __4,175__ and __4,270__
   Their average is __4,222.5__
   Guess: 4,190 (4,220) 4,260
   Clue: higher

G. It is between __4,220__ and __4,270__
   Their average is __4,245__
   Guess: 4,221 4,230 (4,240)
   Clue: lower

H. It is between __4,220__ and __4,240__
   Their average is __4,230__
   Guess (4,230) 4,235 4,239
   Clue: lower

I. It is between __4,220__ and __4,230__
   Their average is __4,225__
   Guess (4,225) 4,227 4,229
   Clue: lower

J. It is between __4,220__ and __4,225__
   Their average is __4,222.5__
   Guess: 4,220 4,221 (4,223)
   Clue: higher

K. It is between __4,223__ and __4,225__
   The number is __4,224__

p. 14 — Operating Room
A. 34; (7 + 3) x 9
B. 14; (15 ÷ 5) + (4 x 2)
C. 12; 6 + (30 ÷ 10) − 7
D. 7; (9 ÷ 3 + 12) ÷ 3
E. 24; 1 + (3 x 11) − 5
F. 13; (21 ÷ 3 + 1) x 6
G. 0; (25 x 2) − (2 x 12)
H. (5 + 5) ÷ 5 + 5
I. (5 x 5 + 5) ÷ 5
J. (5 ÷ 5) x (5 + 5)
K. (5 x 5 x 5) + 5
L. (5 + 5 + 5) ÷ 5
M. 3 x (4 + 6) ÷ 5 + 7
N. (7 − 6 + 4) x 5 x 3
O. ((4 + 6) ÷ 5 + 7) ÷ 3
P. 5 x 7 − (3 x 4 + 6)
Q. (5 x 4 + 7) ÷ 3 + 6

p. 15 — Roman Numerals
A. CCCLXV	B. MMIII
C. DCCXCVI	D. DCCCXLVII
E. MDCCXLII	F. MMMCDXCI
G. DCLXXXV	H. MDCCCXXXVIII
I. MMCCCXLV	J. MMMCCCXLV
K. MMDLV	L. CMXLI
M. MDCXVII	N. MMXXXIX
O. MMMCM	P. MCCCLXXX
Q. DCC	R. MMDCCLXXXIX

1–3. Answers will vary.

p. 16 — Inventions
A. 1714	(12)	B. 499 B.C.	(3)
C. 1665 to 1675	(11)	D. 1823	(14)
E. 250	(4)	F. 1656	(10)
G. 1614	(6)	H. 1879	(15)
I. 1637	(7)	J. 1640	(8)
K. 1642	(9)	L. 2600 B.C.	(1)
M. 1593	(5)	N. 699 B.C.	(2)
O. 1735	(13)		

p. 17 — Charting Roman Numerals
Roman Numeral	Standard Form	Expanded Form	Number Sentence Standard Numerals	Number Sentence Roman Numerals
IX	9	9		
XXII	22	20 + 2	ANSWERS WILL VARY.	
DLXXIV	574	500 + 70 + 4		
XLVI	46	40 + 6		
XCIII	93	90 + 3		
MMCDXVIII	2,418	2000 + 400 + 10 + 8		
CDIX	409	400 + 9		
XXXVI	36	30 + 6		
CMLXXIV	974	900 + 70 + 4		
MMDCIX	2609	2000 + 600 + 9		
DCCXLVII	747	700 + 40 + 7		
XCIX	99	90 + 9		
MMMCDXXXIX	3439	3000 + 400 + 30 + 9		
CCCXCII	392	300 + 90 + 2		
LVI	56	50 + 6		
MMCDXXXIX	2439	2000 + 400 + 30 + 9		
CMXVIII	918	900 + 10 + 8		
MDCCLXXXIV	1784	1000 + 700 + 80 + 4		

p. 18 — Roman Time
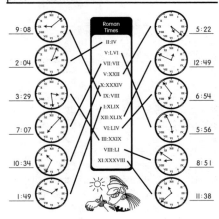

9:08 2:04 3:29 7:07 10:34 1:49

Roman Times
II:IV
V:LVI
VII:VII
V:XXII
X:XXXIV
IX:VIII
I:XLIX
XII:XLIX
VI:LIV
III:XXIX
VIII:LI
XI:XXXVIII

5:22 12:49 6:54 5:56 8:51 11:38

p. 19 — Way Big Amusement Park
Answers will vary.

p. 20 — Good Night
Name	Time to Bed	Time Up	Time in Bed
Jesma	9:30	7:30	10 hours
Sirdo	9:00	6:30	9.5 hours
Judy	8:45	7:30	10.75 hours
Dillon	9:00	7:00	10 hours
Melina	10:00	6:30	8.5 hours
Jen	9:30	7:45	10.25 hours
Rebecca	9:15	6:30	9.25 hours
Omarha	10:00	7:45	9.75 hours
Sydney	11:00	7:00	8 hours
Armani	10:30	7:30	9 hours

Remaining rows in chart will vary.
Graph and statements will also vary.

p. 21 — Card Golf
Meg Ian Jill

Hand 1:
Total: 18 Total: 10 Total: -2
Running total: 36 Running total: 41 Running total: 14

Hand 2:
Total: 9 Total: 13 Total: 1
Running total: 27 Running total: 31 Running total: -1

Hand 3:
Total: 9 Total: -2 Total: 5
Running total: 36 Running total: 21 Running total: 4

Hand 4:
Total: -2 Total: -2 Total: 14
Running total: 34 Running total: 19 Running total: 18

Hand 5:
Total: -2 Total: 1 Total: 9
Running total: 34 Running total: 20 Running total: 16

Hand 6:
Total: 16 Total: 7 Total: 7
Running total: 50 Running total: 48 Running total: 23

Hand 7:
Total: 21 Total: -2 Total: 7
Running total: 48 Running total: 69 Running total: 21

Hand 8:
Total: -6 Total: 2 Total: 2
Running total: 42 Running total: 71 Running total: 23

Hand 9:
Total: 3 Total: 9 Total: 1
Running total: 45 Running total: 80 Running total: 25

The player with the lowest score wins. Who won? __Jill won with 25 points.__

p. 22 — Algebra Challenge

$c = 9$; $e = 3$; $q = 2$; $u = 4$; $y = 6$

$o = 7$; $w = 2$; $x = 3$; $z = 6$

$j = 3$; $p = 4$; $s = 1$; $t = 7$

$b = 4$; $f = 2$; $g = 8$; $k = 6$

$a = 5$; $d = 6$; $h = 1$; $m = 3$; $r = 2$

$d = 2$; $i = 8$; $l = 3$; $n = 1$; $v = 5$

p. 23 — Those Romans!

1. 129 + 180 = 309   CCCIX
2. 401 − 251 = 150   CL
3. 601 − 417 = 184   CLXXXIV
4. 477 + 279 = 756   DCCLVI
5. 284 + 308 = 592   DXCII
6. 591 − 163 = 428   CDXXVIII
7. 391 + 159 = 550   DL
8. 932 − 555 = 377   CCCLXXVII
9. 216 + 668 = 884   DCCCLXXXIV
10. 926 − 219 = 707   DCCVII
11. 726 + 249 = 975   CMLXXV
12. 384 − 77 = 307   CCCVII

p. 24 — Values

A. 50,000	B. 800	C. 2
D. 7,000	E. 200,000	F. 70
G. 2,000	H. 10	I. 400,000
J. 8	K. 60,000	L. 300
M. 600,000	N. 10,000	O. 3
P. 0	Q. 20	R. 1,000
S. 257,872	T. 462,318	U. 611,023

1. 515,744
2. 720,190
3. 868,895
4. 1,073,341
5. 1,222,046
6. 1,331,213
7. 500,000 + 10,000 + 5,000 + 700 + 40 + 4
8. 700,000 + 20,000 + 100 + 90 + 1
9. 800,000 + 60,000 + 8,000 + 800 + 90 + 5
10. 1,000,000 + 70,000 + 3,000 + 300 + 40 + 1
11. 1,000,000 + 200,000 + 20,000 + 2,000 + 40 + 6
12. 1,000,000 + 300,000 + 30,000 + 1,000 + 200 + 10 + 3

p. 25 — Cross Patch

Across

A.
```
  2631448
   749213
  4930406
     2781
+  198364
 8,512,212
```
B.
```
   463951
   293466
  1889423
     7992
+   36483
 2,691,315
```
C.
```
  3526808
     9426
  1745971
  1268319
+  174550
 6,725,074
```

Down

D.
```
  2331403
   566987
    26825
  1009743
+  631618
 4,566,576
```
E.
```
   486092
  1645357
     7806
  2492534
+ 1629865
 6,261,654
```
F.
```
    48932
  2192443
   707527
   145869
+    6403
 3,101,174
```

Across

A.
```
    45736
  2603481
   826018
  3469752
+    6435
 6,951,422
```
B.
```
  7062495
    93246
   528793
  1844631
+  264868
 9,794,033
```
C.
```
  4625191
  2930467
   298154
  1008479
+   64827
 8,927,118
```

Down

Write three addition problems with five addends each. The sums must fit in the puzzle.

D.   E.   F.

Answers will vary.

p. 26 — Addition Boxes

A.
```
  6549
+ 7372
 13921
```
B.
```
  5498
+ 4672
 10170
```
C.
```
  6546
+ 2797
  9343
```
D.
```
  3168
+ 5738
  8906
```
E.
```
  764925
+ 189342
  954267
```
F.
```
  274173
+ 489256
  763429
```
G.
```
  231174
+ 582968
  814142
```
H.
```
  389442
+ 958318
 1347760
```
I.
```
  418360
+  62753
  481113
```

p. 27 — More Addition Boxes

A.
```
  753292
  128451
+ 455289
 1337578
```
B.
```
  192446
  396563
+ 477435
 1066444
```
C.
```
  628306
  838932
+ 461626
 1928864
```
D.
```
  273728
  953793
+ 416728
 1644394
```
E.
```
     2809
      465
     5689
       81
     5138
+    3038
  120692
```
F.
```
     5567
     2869
     5622
     8311
      632
     3128
+     746
   76993
```
G.
```
     6272
     1916
      972
     2172
     6200
     1704
+    2681
   99428
```
H.
```
     789256
      24578
       2087
     804277
+       485
   1845659
```

Try two additional problems of your own. Check your answers with a calculator.

p. 28 — Missing Digits

A.
```
  576832
+ 674936
 1251768
```
B.
```
  237194
+ 863593
 1100787
```
C.
```
  763551
- 483493
  280058
```
D.
```
  492069
- 256175
  235894
```
E.
```
  560702
- 239843
  320859
```
F.
```
  932568
+ 580275
 1512843
```
G.
```
   541872
+  129679
   671551
```
H.
```
   160091
-  128364
   031727
```
I.
```
   724826
-  182749
   542077
```
J.
```
   495726
+  382197
   877923
```
K.
```
   264160
-  134692
   129468
```
L.
```
   389456
+  293885
   683341
```
M.
```
   443013
-  273784
   169829
```
N.
```
   500201
-  314344
   185855
```
O.
```
   906430
-  342642
   563788
```
P.
```
   379253
   526483
+  113562
  1019298
```
Q.
```
   376530
   152847
+  203644
   733021
```
R.
```
   484785
   723154
+  627673
  1835612
```

p. 30 — Thermometer

1. 8,733,032
2. 9,469,739
3. 11,101,719
4. 6,133,400
5. 6,864,758
6. 4,155,189
7. 6,750,149
8. 6,862,296
9. 1,391,068
10. 3,974,633
11. 3,244,600
12. 6,312,077

GABRIEL FAHRENHEIT

p. 31 — Hourglass

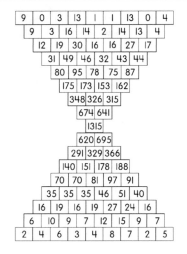

9	0	3	13	1	1	13	0	4

```
 9  3 16 14  2 14 13  4
 12 19 30 16 16 27 17
  31 49 46 32 43 44
   80 95 78 75 87
   175 173 153 162
     348 326 315
       674 641
         1315
        620 695
       291 329 366
     140 151 178 188
     70 70 81 97 91
   35 35 35 46 51 40
  16 16 19 27 24 16
 6 10 9 7 12 15 9 7
2 4 6 3 4 8 7 2 5
```

p. 32 — Give It a Loan

A. 408	B. 763
C. 381	D. 207; 577 − 370
E. 357; 658 − 301	F. 383; 686 − 303

G. 524; Add 3 to both; 854 − 330
H. 80; Add 50 to both; 985 − 905
I. 351; Add 40 to both; 654 − 303

p. 33 — Multiple Loans

A. 474

B. 219

C. 66; Add 5 to both; 326 − 260; Add 40 to both; 366 − 300

D. 153; Add 1 to both; 433 − 280; Add 20 to both; 453 − 300

E. 2555; Add 4 to both; 3105 − 550; Add 50 to both; 3155 − 600

F. 4068; Add 6 to both; 9938 − 5870; Add 30 to both; 9968 − 5900

G. 737; Add 2 to both; 9367 − 8630; Add 400 to both; 9767 − 9030

H. 4047; Add 5 to both; 5637 − 1590; Add 10 to both; 5647 − 1600

p. 34 — Zero Land

A. 45,498	B. 3,759
C. 24,633	D. 37,431
E. 47,366	F. 275,194
G. 337,602	H. 162,055
I. 177,759	J. 576,112
K. 167,728	L. 375,388

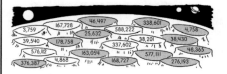

p. 35 — Make That Number

Answers will vary.

CD-4335 *Brain-Boosting Math*

p. 36 — Color by Number

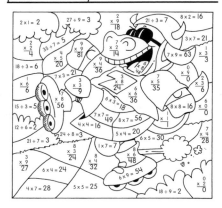

p. 38 — Fooling You

Algebraic Expression	Expression in Words
$g - 9$	nine less than g
$k \div 5$	k divided by five
$v + 5$	v and five
$y - 7$	y decreased by seven
$6s$	six times s
$12 \div j$	twelve divided by j
$15 - t$	t less than fifteen
$20 + c$	twenty more than c
$12e$	12 times e
$w + 34$	w plus 34
$36 \div m$	36 divided by m
$q - 6$	6 less than q
$n - 3$	3 less than n
$7z$	7 times z
$17 + f$	17 more than f

Solve the expressions for each given value.

$5t$		$10,200 - m$		$1,500 \div j$		$x + 97,846$	
t	Answer	m	Answer	j	Answer	x	Answer
3	15	6,328	3,872	50	30	26,423	124,269
90	450	9,004	1,196	2	750	84,532	182,378
22	110	2,561	7,639	25	60	36,274	134,120
500	2,500	3,264	6,936	14	107 R2	57,647	155,493
15	75	10,133	67	32	46 R28	14,925	112,711

p. 39 — Arrangement

A. $12 \div 3 \times 4 \div 2 - 6 \times 5 = 10$
B. $6 + 9 \div 3 \times 5 - 1 \div 8 = 3$
C. $7 + 2 + 5 \div 7 \times 1 + 3 = 5$
D. $8 + 2 \div 5 \times 4 + 7 \div 3 = 5$
E. $9 \times 3 - 2 \div 5 \times 4 + 1 \div 7 = 3$
F. $3 \times 9 - 7 \div 5 + 2 \times 4 \div 8 = 3$
G–I. Answers will vary.

p. 40 — Back and Forth

A. MMCDLVI
B. DCCCXCIV
C. DCXXVIII
D. MCDVI
E. MMML
F. LXIX
G. MMCCXLVII
H. MMMCDXLIV
I. 1960; MCMLX
J. 2576; MMDLXXVI
K. 3479; MMMCDLXXIX
L. 901; CMI
M. 1730; MDCCXXX
N. 2975; MMCMLXXV
O. 2508; MMDVIII
P. 2763; MMDCCLXIII
1. 465
2. 2530
3. 1642
4. 99
5. 3162
6. 257
7. 2888
8. 1034
9. 1005
10. 3493
11. MMMCMXCIX (3999)
12. Answers will vary.

p. 41 — Place Value Drawing

A. $\begin{array}{r} 1351 \\ \times\ 7 \\ \hline 9,457 \end{array}$ = __0__ ten thousands, __9__ thousands, __4__ hundreds, __5__ tens, __7__ ones

B. $\begin{array}{r} 262 \\ \times\ 32 \\ \hline 8,384 \end{array}$ = __0__ ten thousands, __8__ thousands, __3__ hundreds, __8__ tens, __4__ ones

C. $\begin{array}{r} 19 \\ \times\ 54 \\ \hline 1,026 \end{array}$ = __0__ ten thousands, __1__ thousands, __0__ hundreds, __2__ tens, __6__ ones

D. $\begin{array}{r} 423 \\ \times\ 215 \\ \hline 90,945 \end{array}$ = __9__ ten thousands, __0__ thousands, __9__ hundreds, __4__ tens, __5__ ones

pp. 42–43 — Breaking Apart

A. $\begin{array}{r} 75 \\ \times\ 29 \end{array}$
$9 \times 5 =$	45
$9 \times 70 =$	630
$20 \times 5 =$	100
$20 \times 70 =$	+1400
	2,175

B. $\begin{array}{r} 92 \\ \times\ 33 \end{array}$
$3 \times 2 =$	6
$3 \times 90 =$	270
$30 \times 2 =$	60
$30 \times 90 =$	+2700
	3,036

C. $\begin{array}{r} 35 \\ \times\ 26 \end{array}$
$6 \times 5 =$	30
$6 \times 30 =$	180
$20 \times 5 =$	100
$20 \times 30 =$	+600
	910

D. $\begin{array}{r} 1620 \\ \times\ 9 \end{array}$
$9 \times 0 =$	0
$9 \times 20 =$	180
$9 \times 600 =$	5400
$9 \times 1000 =$	+9000
	14,580

E. $\begin{array}{r} 2561 \\ \times\ 4 \end{array}$
$4 \times 1 =$	4
$4 \times 60 =$	240
$4 \times 500 =$	2000
$4 \times 2000 =$	+8000
	10,244

F. $\begin{array}{r} 4059 \\ \times\ 6 \end{array}$
$6 \times 9 =$	54
$6 \times 50 =$	300
$6 \times 0 =$	0
$6 \times 4000 =$	+24000
	24,354

G. $\begin{array}{r} 547 \\ \times\ 32 \end{array}$
$2 \times 7 =$	14
$2 \times 40 =$	80
$2 \times 500 =$	1000
$30 \times 7 =$	210
$30 \times 40 =$	1200
$30 \times 500 =$	+15000
	17,504

H. $\begin{array}{r} 333 \\ \times\ 14 \end{array}$
$4 \times 3 =$	12
$4 \times 30 =$	120
$4 \times 300 =$	1200
$10 \times 3 =$	30
$10 \times 30 =$	300
$10 \times 300 =$	+3000
	4,662

7,293   52,020   299,222   81,918

The simpler problems used to find the products in I–R may vary.

I. $\begin{array}{r} 56 \\ \times\ 27 \end{array}$
$7 \times 56 =$	392
$20 \times 56 =$	+1120
	1,512

J. $\begin{array}{r} 85 \\ \times\ 71 \end{array}$
$1 \times 85 =$	85
$70 \times 85 =$	+5950
	6,035

K. $\begin{array}{r} 69 \\ \times\ 13 \end{array}$
$3 \times 69 =$	207
$10 \times 69 =$	+690
	897

L. $\begin{array}{r} 46 \\ \times\ 38 \end{array}$
$8 \times 46 =$	368
$30 \times 46 =$	+1380
	1,748

M. $\begin{array}{r} 243 \\ \times\ 61 \end{array}$
$61 \times 3 =$	183
$61 \times 40 =$	2440
$61 \times 200 =$	+12200
	14,823

N. $\begin{array}{r} 156 \\ \times\ 26 \end{array}$
$26 \times 6 =$	156
$26 \times 50 =$	1300
$26 \times 100 =$	+2600
	4,056

O. $\begin{array}{r} 422 \\ \times\ 57 \end{array}$
$57 \times 2 =$	114
$57 \times 20 =$	1140
$57 \times 400 =$	+22800
	24,054

P. $\begin{array}{r} 854 \\ \times\ 14 \end{array}$
$14 \times 4 =$	56
$14 \times 50 =$	700
$14 \times 800 =$	+11200
	11,956

Q. $\begin{array}{r} 625 \\ \times\ 138 \end{array}$
$8 \times 625 =$	5000
$30 \times 625 =$	18750
$100 \times 625 =$	+62500
	86,250

R. $\begin{array}{r} 709 \\ \times\ 483 \end{array}$
$3 \times 709 =$	2127
$80 \times 709 =$	56720
$400 \times 709 =$	+283600
	342,447

p. 44 — Multiplication Boxes

A. $\begin{array}{r} 92 \\ \times\ 47 \end{array}$ → 4 3 2 4

B. $\begin{array}{r} 54 \\ \times\ 26 \end{array}$ → 1 4 0 4

C. $\begin{array}{r} 61 \\ \times\ 85 \end{array}$ → 5 1 8 5

D. $\begin{array}{r} 946 \\ \times\ 23 \end{array}$ → 2 1 7 5 8

E. $\begin{array}{r} 719 \\ \times\ 15 \end{array}$ → 1 0 7 8 5

F. $\begin{array}{r} 621 \\ \times\ 87 \end{array}$ → 5 4 0 2 7

G. $\begin{array}{r} 489 \\ \times\ 239 \end{array}$ → 1 1 6 8 7 1

H. $\begin{array}{r} 253 \\ \times\ 746 \end{array}$ → 1 8 8 7 3 8

I. $\begin{array}{r} 169 \\ \times\ 815 \end{array}$ → 1 3 7 7 3 5

p. 45 — Pulling It All Together

A. 5,488
B. 18,164
C. 17,466
D. 9,808

p. 46 — Basketball

1. 189,728 (2 points)
2. 101,385 (4 points)
3. 288,822 (2 points)
4. 631,526 (3 points)
5. 296,356 (3 points)
6. 381,921 (3 points)
7. 121,348 (4 points)
8. 28,380 (3 points)
9. 62,928 (2 points)
10. 126,384 (3 points)
11. 88,326 (5 points)
12. 145,332 (3 points)

Odds total: 18 points
Evens total: 19 points
Evens win.

p. 47 — Delicate Operation

A. 1,928,888
$(1 + 9) \div 2 \times 8 + (8 \div 8 + 8) = 49$
B. 878,156
$(8 - 7) \times 8 + (1 + 5) \times 6 = 44$
C. 320,190
$(3 \times 2 + 0 - 1) \times 9 - 0 = 45$
D. 810,390
$(8 + 1 - 0) \div 3 \times 9 - 0 = 27$
E. 997,866
$9 \times 9 - 7 \times 8 + 6 \times 6 = 61$
F. 541,206
$(5 \times 4 \div (1 \times 2) + 0) \times 6 = 60$
G. 3,249,668
$[(3 + 2 - 4) \times 9 \times 6 - 6] \div 8 = 6$
H. 1,197,027
$(1 + 1 + 9 + 7 + 0) \div 2 \times 7 = 63$
I. Number sentences will vary but must use all the digits in the answer: 1,632,288.

p. 48 — Pyramid

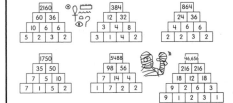

p. 49 — Multiplication Hourglass

Answers will vary.

pp. 50–51 — Speeding Tickets

Name (Initials)	Posted Speed Limit	Speed	Fine Adjustment	Miles Per Hour Over the Speed Limit	Fine
GWW	35	50		15 mph	$175
JKF	55	82		27 mph	$390
ENP	45	63		18 mph	$220
CGH	45	94		49 mph	$830
MMJ	25	31	**	6 mph	$180
SAE	40	62		22 mph	$290
MRC	25	59		34 mph	$530
DTP	15	34	**	19 mph	$705
FEG	15	41	**	26 mph	$1,110
DBF	55	67	*	12 mph	$260
KLO	35	44		9 mph	$90

pp. 50–51 — Speeding Tickets (continued)
1. FEG
2. KLO
3. $1,020
4. $434.55
5. $290
6. 49 mph
7. 6 mph
8. 43 mph
9. 21.54 mph
10. 19 mph
11. No. FEG was only going 26 mph over the speed limit but was in a school zone. The fine was tripled.
12. No. MMJ was going the least over the speed limit but the fine was tripled.
13. 22.2 (23) weeks
14. $72.50
15. 5 weeks
16. Answers will vary.

p. 52 — How Many in Each Group?
A. 687 R3
B. 82 R12
C. 143
D. 221

p. 53 — Repeated Subtraction
Subtractable pieces used to find solution will vary.
A. 66
B. 231
C. 3617 R4
D. 69 R39
E. 99 R8
F. 95 R18
G. 118 R26
H. 132 R67
I. 2870 R20
J. 377 R93
K. 2104 R35
L. 6251 R4

p. 54 — Elements of Math

E	U	C	L	I	D

6,215 R3 8,938 R3 9,064 R3 9,603 R3 12,367 R3 13,375 R3

p. 55 — Box It
A. 2,617
B. 1,982
C. 7,481
D. 7,516
E. 2,475
F. 4,895
G. 5,026
H. 6,840
Both grids are correct.

2	4	7	5
6	8	4	0
1	9	8	2
7	5	1	6

2	6	1	7
4	8	9	5
7	4	8	1
5	0	2	6

p. 56 — Division Venn
A. 1820 R8
B. 1055 R42
C. 285 R73
D. 478 R62
E. 608 R74
F. 563 R5
G. 899 R12
H. 642 R80
I. 438 R53
J. 335 R16
K. 908 R16
L. 464 R3

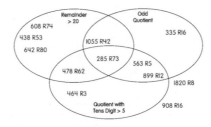

p. 57 — Economics Project
1. 12.5 pins
2. 10,500 beads
3. 20 bags
4. $50
5. 13 packs
6. $7.80
7. $57.80
8. 21¢
9. $35.95 (62%); $54.70 (95%); $73.45 (127%)

p. 58 — Big Sale

Item	Regular Price	Days 1–5 10% off	Days 6–10 15% off	Days 11–15 20% off	Days 16–20 25% off	Days 21–25 50% off	Days 26–30 75% off
Trading Cards	$3.75	$3.38	$3.19	$3.00	$2.81	$1.88	$0.94
Game Cartridge	$38.99	$35.09	$33.14	$31.19	$29.24	$19.50	$9.75
CD	$23.00	$20.70	$19.55	$18.40	$17.25	$11.50	$5.75
Movie Figures	$19.99	$17.99	$16.99	$15.99	$14.99	$10.00	$5.00
Soccer Ball	$26.25	$23.63	$22.31	$21.00	$19.69	$13.13	$6.56

Answers will vary.
1. No. Prices are not reduced much.
2. Last two sets of 5 days
3. Wait until it is 50% or 75% off.
4. Buy one now before they are gone.
5. Wait until it is cheaper.
6. Buy it right away.

p. 59 — Totem Pole

1. nine point zero zero six / ninety-one point two zero two / two hundred fifty-eight point nine zero one	9.006 / 91.202 / + 258.901 / 359.109	3
2. five hundred four point zero three / point zero nine seven / ninety-one point zero five six	504.03 / .097 / + 91.056 / 595.183	2
3. point four nine eight / twelve point six five eight / three hundred point nine	498 / 12.658 / + 300.9 / 314.056	4
4. one hundred twenty-four point zero zero three / sixteen point one four six / six hundred five point zero zero nine	124.003 / 16.146 / + 605.009 / 745.158	1
5. one point zero zero two / three point zero zero nine / eighty point zero six five	1.002 / 3.009 / + 80.065 / 84.076	8
6. twenty-one point zero two three / one point nine eight four / seventy-eight point three	21.023 / 1.984 / + 78.3 / 101.307	7
7. point eight zero four / two hundred twenty-four point eight / three point zero zero four	.804 / 224.8 / + 3.004 / 228.608	6
8. two hundred thirty-one point zero two / sixty-four point eight five one / point zero four eight	231.02 / 64.851 / + .048 / 295.919	5

p. 60 — Discovering Diamonds
A. 315.6846 — emerald
B. 181.131 — ruby
C. 141 — diamond
D. 602.5966
E. 479.2301 — ruby
F. 378.6754 — emerald
G. 564.5139
H. 818.7194
I. 25.5223 — topaz
J. 269.5565
K. 70 — diamond
L. 515.3726 — topaz

p. 61 — Just Jousting
Answers are listed from greatest to least.
1. *22.805   17.707   5.098
2. *22.917   13.978   8.939
3. *22.656   21.078   1.578
4. *17.26   12.445   4.815
5. *27.521   14.74   12.781

p. 62 — Start Where You Left Off
A. 399.94
B. 375.934
C. 106.11
D. 113
E. 67.38
F. 57.58
G. 87.36
H. 141.13
I. 85.04
J. 56.76
K. 65.945
L. 84.415
M. 83.777
N. 145.8
O. 116.38
P. 99.378
Q. 104.108
R. 24.648
S. 32.25
T. 45.7

p. 63 — Decimal Diagram
A. 2462.62
B. 24.05
C. 986.28
D. 687.879
E. 21975.15
F. 982.8
G. 541.26
H. 18.54
I. 31.1695
J. 75.138
K. 36.725
L. 1687.672
M. 719.3928

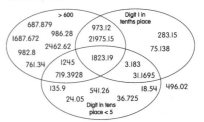

p. 64 — Pick Those Books
1. 2 at $1.95 each
2. 1 at $1.50, 1 at $2.95
3. 1 at $1.95, 1 at $5.95, 1 at $7.95
4. 2 at $3.95, 1 at $1.95, 1 at $1.50
5. 2 at $3.95, 1 at $2.95
6. 4 at $3.95, 1 at $5.95
7. 1 at $0.95, 1 at $1.50, 1 at $2.95
8. 2 at $1.95, 1 at $0.95
9. 1 at $9.95, 3 at $0.95
10. 3 at $3.95, 1 at $5.95, 1 at $9.95
11. 3 at $2.95, 2 at $0.95, 2 at $1.95, 1 at $4.95

p. 65 — Swedish Scientist
A. 7.1
B. 11.2
C. 9.08
D. 62.02
E. 21.7
F. 37.5
G. 16.9
H. 28.13
I. 38.37
J. 21.6
K. 12.3
L. 10.7

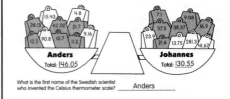

What is the first name of the Swedish scientist who invented the Celsius thermometer scale? ___Anders___

CD-4335 *Brain-Boosting Math*

p. 66 — I Only Want One
1. 6¢
2. 26¢
3. 7¢
4. 11¢
5. 15¢; 35¢
6. 31¢; 44¢
7. 8¢; 8¢
8. 12¢; 13¢

p. 67 — Fooling You with Decimals

Algebraic Expression	Expression in Words
$16.4 \div j$	sixteen point four divided by j
$v + 6.1$	v and six point one
$2.4s$	two point four times s
$k \div .05$	k divided by point zero five
$.51 - t$	t less than point five one
$g - 8.4$	eight point four less than g
$5.06 + h$	five point zero six more than h
$y - 11.37$	y decreased by eleven point three seven
$30.03z$	thirty point zero three times z
$w + 9.6$	w plus nine point six
$q - 8.18$	eight point one eight less than q
$1.02e$	one point zero two times e
$n - 1.45$	one point four five less than n
$14.87 + j$	fourteen point eight seven more than j
$.09 \div m$	point zero nine divided by m

$.3r$		$2.041 + e$		$9.09 \div w$		$f - 9.903$	
r	Answer	e	Answer	w	Answer	f	Answer
1.5	.45	56.72	58.761	2	45.45	11.04	1.137
2	.6	7.306	9.347	3	3.03	22.7	12.797
.08	.024	781.4	783.441	.06	151.5	64.95	55.047
4.7	1.41	9.95	11.991	1.2	7.575	11.453	1.55
9.02	2.706	.679	2.72	.001	9090	10.861	.958

p. 68 — Rounding Power
A. 3,200; 3.2×10^3
B. 6,390; 6.39×10^3
C. 90,250; 9.025×10^4
D. 9,153,000; 9.153×10^6
E. 52,800; 5.28×10^4
F. 293,100; 2.931×10^5
G. 7,483,000; 7.483×10^6
H. 336,000; 3.36×10^5
I. 720,000; 7.2×10^5
J. 1,300,000; 1.3×10^6
K. 700,000; 7×10^5
L. 5,000; 5×10^3
M. 82,720,000; 8.272×10^7
N. 8,500; 8.5×10^3
O. 47,200; 4.72×10^4
P. 3,000; 3×10^3

p. 69 — Assessing Shapes
1. Yes
2. No
3. Yes
4. Yes
5. Yes
6. Yes
7. Yes
8. No
9. No
10. No
11. Yes
12. No
13. Yes
14. Yes
15. No
16. Yes
17. Yes
18. Yes
19. Yes
20. No
21. Yes
22. No
23. Yes
24. Yes
25. Yes
Drawings will vary.

p. 70 — Measuring Angles
1. acute; angle ABC; 70°
2. right; angle GET; 90°
3. acute; angle THE; 85°
4. obtuse; angle FAT; 175°
5. acute; angle HOW; 15°
6. obtuse; angle BAG; 110°
7. right; angle ARE; 90°
8. obtuse; angle POP; 190°
9. acute; angle CAN; 45°
10. acute; angle TEN; 30°
11. obtuse; angle PAY; 135°
12. right; angle SIX; 90°
Figures will vary.

p. 71 — Making Angles
Angles drawn must meet criteria given.
Figures will vary.

p. 72 — Polygons
1. quadrilateral GRAB
2. angle RGB
3. angle BAR
4. angle GBA
5. GR = 3cm; RA = 4 cm; AB = 2.9 cm;
   BG = 2.3 cm
6. RA; 4 cm
7. 12.2 cm
8. hexagon ABCDEF
9. angle BAF or angle ABC
10. angle AFE
11. angle DEF
12. AF; 5.5 cm
13. AF = 5.5 cm; FE = 1 cm; ED = 2 cm;
    DC = 2 cm; CB = 4.7 cm; BA = 3 cm
14. 18.2 cm
15. pentagon MNOPQ
16. angle OPQ
17. angle NOP
18. angles MQP, MNO
19. MQ = 4.5 cm; QP = 1.3 cm;
    PO = 5 cm; ON = 2 cm; NM = 3 cm
20. OP; 5 cm
21. 15.8 cm
22. triangle SIX
23. angle SXI
24. angle XIS
25. SI = 6.3 cm; IX = 5 cm; XS = 2 cm
26. SI; 6.3 cm
27. 13.3 cm

p. 73 — Make the Shape
Drawings will vary.
1. No. A rectangle has four 90° angles.
3. No. A right triangle has one right angle
   and two acute angles.
4. No. All three angles must add up to
   180°.

p. 74 — Album Areas
1. 8 photos
2. 6 photos
3–6. Answers will vary.

p. 75 — Zoo Homes
1. a. 3,900 cubic feet   b. 1,510 square feet
2. a. 2,304 cubic in.   b. 1,152 square in.
3. a. 56 cubic feet   b. 100 square feet
4. a. 24,360 cubic centimeters
   b. 5,972 square centimeters
5. a. 3,744 cubic meters
   b. 1,536 square meters

p. 76 — Storage Containers
Answers will vary.

p. 77 — Here to There
1. 1-8/16 inches; 6-5/16 inches
2. 4-13/16 inches   3. Answers will vary.
4. 5.8 cm; 17.4 cm   5. 11.6 cm
6. Answers will vary.
7. a. yellow   b. yellow   c. red
   d. green   e. yellow   f. red
   g. red   h. green   i. green
   j. red   k. red   l. red
8. c, f, l, k, g, j, a, e , b, h, i, d

pp. 78–79 — Measure This
A. p = 12 cm; a = 6 square cm
B. p = 16 cm; a = 10 square cm
C. p = 7 cm; a = 3 square cm
D. d = 6 cm; r = 3 cm; c = 19 cm;
   a = 28 square cm
E. d = 3 cm; r = 1.5 cm; c = 9 cm;
   a = 7 square cm
F. p = 16 cm; a = 12 square cm
G. p = 18 cm; a = 20 square cm
H. d = 5 cm; a = 2.5 cm; c = 16 cm;
   a = 20 square cm
I. p = 13 cm; a = 8 square cm
J. p = 12 cm; a = 9 square cm
K. p = 11.5 cm; a = 6 square cm
L. d = 4 cm; r = 2 cm; c = 13 cm;
   a = 13 sqare cm
M. p = 18.1 cm; a = 15 square cm
N. p = 21 cm; a = 18 square cm
O. p = 17.3 cm; a = 12 square cm
1. parallelogram area = 70;
   rectangle area = 2; triangle area = 6;
   circle area = 3.14
   70 – (2 + 6 + 3.14) = 58.86
                       or 59 square cm
2. 66.86 square cm; 64 square cm;
   68 square cm
3. 9.14 square cm
4. 5.14 square cm

p. 80 — Mail It
1. less than 1 ounce; 37¢
2. between 1 and 2 ounces (1.6 oz.); $2.40
3. less than 1.2 ounces; 37¢ or 60¢
4. between 2.2 and 2.8 ounces; 83¢
5. between 1 and 1.2 ounces; 60¢
6. .8 ounces each; 37¢ to send each
7. 3 weigh 1 ounce, 2 weigh 1.5 ounces;
   37¢ each to send 3, 60¢ each to send 2
   for total of $2.31

p. 81 — Navigating the Waters
Answers will vary but need to follow
restrictions and be written in correct
coordinates.

p. 82 — Temperature Tales
Answers will vary but must show an understanding of the relationship between temperature and function.

p. 83 — Density Columns
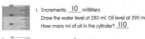
1. Increments: _10_ milliliters
Draw the water level at 280 ml. Oil level at 390 ml.
How many ml of oil in the cylinder? _110_

2. Increments: _1_ milliliters
Draw the corn syrup level at 32 ml. Water level at 38 ml. Oil level at 46 ml.
How many ml of water? _6_   oil? _8_

3. Increments: _2_ milliliters
Draw the corn syrup level at 122 ml. Water level at 130 ml. Oil level at 134 ml.
How many ml of water? _8_   oil? _4_   corn syrup? _122_

4. Increments: _5_ milliliters
Draw the corn syrup level at 45 ml. Water level at 75 ml. Oil level at 90 ml.
How many ml of corn syrup? _45_   oil? _15_   water? _30_

5. Increments: _20_ milliliters
Draw the corn syrup level at 440. Water level at 940 ml. Oil level at 1220.
How many ml of oil? _280_   corn syrup? _440_   water? _500_

6. Increments: _50_ milliliters
Draw the corn syrup level at 50. Water level at 150 ml. Oil level at 200.
How many ml of oil? _50_   water? _100_   corn syrup? _50_

7. Increments: _5_ milliliters
Draw the corn syrup level at 7. Water level at 11 ml. Oil level at 18.
How many ml of oil? _7_   water? _4_   corn syrup? _7_

p. 84 — Draw the Fractions
Other answers are possible.
1. 3 yellow, 2 green, 1 orange
2. 4 red, 7 yellow, 3 blue
3. 8 white, 3 yellow, 1 other
4. 3 orange, 8 green, 12 blue, 1 other
5. 2 blue, 5 yellow, 3 other
6. 6 red, 6 black, 6 yellow
7–8. Answers will vary.

p. 85 — Draw This
Other answers are possible.
1. 4 dimes, 5 pennies, 1 nickel; 50¢
2. 3 quarters, 4 nickels, 2 dimes, 3 pennies; $1.18
3. 20 pennies, 10 nickels, 4 half-dollars, 6 dimes; $3.30
4. 4 nickels, 10 quarters, 5 dimes, 1 penny; $3.21
5. 6 pennies, 3 quarters, 1 nickel, 1 dime, 1 half-dollar; $1.46
6. 1 quarter, 9 nickels, 3 pennies, 2 dimes, 1 half-dollar; $1.43

p. 86 — Coin Fractions
1. a. 4/24 or 1/6; b. 7/24; c. 6/24 or 1/4; d. 5/24; e. 2/24 or 1/12
2. a. 2 half-dollars, 4 quarters, 2 dimes, 2 nickels, 2 pennies
   b. 2 half-dollars, 5 quarters, 2 dimes, 3 nickels
   c. 1 quarter, 4 dimes, 5 nickels, 2 pennies
3. 2 half-dollars, 5 quarters, 4 dimes, 5 nickels, 2 pennies
4. 3 quarters, 1 nickel
5–6. Answers will vary.

p. 87 — Fraction Riddles
1. 14 blocks
2. 49 crackers
3. 25 stars
4. 153 pretzels
5. 12 cupcakes
6. 132 crayons
7. 132 calories
8. 24 coins
A–C. Answers will vary.

p. 88 — Gone Fishing
1. 72 sand fleas
2. 18 sand fleas
3. 54 hits
4. 36 reeled in
5. 20 whiting
6. 6 pompano
7. 9 sheepshead
8. 1 sea bass
9. 24 fish kept; 12 fish thrown back
10. 12 fish
11. 2 fish
12. 4 fish
13. 2 deep-fried
    2 fried with butter and lemon
14. 1 fish
15. 5 fish

p. 89 — What Time?
1. 3:05
2. 3:20
3. 12:30
4. 4:20
5. 5:05
6. 6:30
7. 3:01
8. 3:42
9. 8:28
10. 3:44

p. 90 — Tic-Tac-Toe Fractions
Write each fraction in lowest terms.
Draw an X on these reduced fractions in the grids.
A. $\frac{6}{9} = \frac{2}{3}$ B. $\frac{3}{18} = \frac{1}{6}$
C. $\frac{5}{20} = \frac{1}{4}$ D. $\frac{24}{30} = \frac{4}{5}$
E. $\frac{10}{16} = \frac{5}{8}$ F. $\frac{24}{42} = \frac{4}{7}$
G. $\frac{28}{63} = \frac{4}{9}$ H. $\frac{21}{33} = \frac{7}{11}$
I. $\frac{15}{18} = \frac{5}{6}$ J. $\frac{15}{35} = \frac{3}{7}$
K. $\frac{4}{36} = \frac{1}{9}$ L. $\frac{5}{40} = \frac{1}{8}$
M. $\frac{8}{28} = \frac{2}{7}$

Draw an O on these reduced fractions in the grids.
N. $\frac{20}{32} = \frac{5}{8}$ O. $\frac{6}{66} = \frac{2}{11}$
P. $\frac{5}{15} = \frac{1}{3}$ Q. $\frac{12}{15} = \frac{4}{5}$
R. $\frac{35}{45} = \frac{7}{9}$ S. $\frac{12}{21} = \frac{4}{7}$
T. $\frac{8}{40} = \frac{1}{5}$ U. $\frac{30}{35} = \frac{6}{7}$
V. $\frac{36}{40} = \frac{9}{10}$ W. $\frac{14}{20} = \frac{7}{10}$
X. $\frac{6}{27} = \frac{2}{9}$ Y. $\frac{4}{10} = \frac{2}{5}$
Z. $\frac{18}{24} = \frac{3}{4}$ AA. $\frac{14}{35} = \frac{2}{5}$

p. 91 — Waterfall

p. 92 — Letter Math
1. add = 1-5/6
2. math = 1-1/3
3. circle = 3
4. square = 3-3/4
5. equal = 3-1/12
6. less = 3
7. tally = 2-5/6
8. graph = 2-5/6
9. table = 2-1/2
10. set = 1-2/3
11. tens = 2-1/2
12. sign = 2-3/4
13. coin = 1-11/12
14. dime = 1-11/12
15. 8/6 + 13/12 + 11/6 = 48/12 = 4-1/4
16–17. Answers will vary.

p. 93 — Three Stars
A. 1/4   B. 1-1/6 or 7/6
C. 3/5   D. 5/6
E. 5/8   F. 1/3
G. 3/4   H. 7/10
I. 4/9   J. 2/7
K. 2/5   L. 2/3
M. 4/7   N. 1/5
O. 7/8   P. 9/10
Q. 3/10   R. 5/7   4 points total

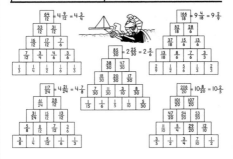

p. 94 — Fraction Pyramid

p. 95 — When Is It One?
When is it one?
WHEN THE DENOMINATOR EQUALS THE NUMERATOR

OPEN MIC NIGHT

p. 96 — Kelp!

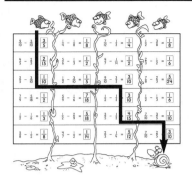

p. 97 — Apple Picking

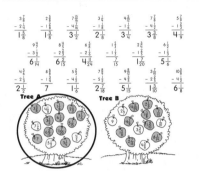

Tree A Tree B

p. 98 — Fraction Venn

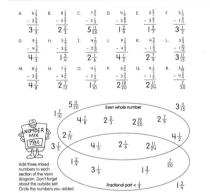

Even whole number

Fractional part < ½

Add three mixed numbers to each section of the Venn diagram. Don't forget about the outside set! Circle the numbers you added.

p. 99 — Greater, Less, or Equal

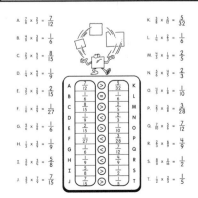

A. $\frac{7}{8} \times \frac{2}{3} = \frac{7}{12}$
K. $\frac{3}{4} \times \frac{5}{8} = \frac{5}{32}$

B. $\frac{4}{9} \times \frac{3}{4} = \frac{1}{3}$
L. $\frac{1}{2} \times \frac{2}{3} = \frac{1}{6}$

C. $\frac{2}{3} \times \frac{4}{5} = \frac{8}{15}$
M. $\frac{3}{5} \times \frac{4}{6} = \frac{2}{5}$

D. $\frac{1}{4} \times \frac{2}{3} = \frac{2}{15}$
N. $\frac{5}{6} \times \frac{4}{5} = \frac{2}{3}$

E. $\frac{2}{3} \times \frac{3}{5} = \frac{2}{15}$
O. $\frac{1}{4} \times \frac{2}{5} = \frac{1}{10}$

F. $\frac{1}{6} \times \frac{2}{9} = \frac{1}{27}$
P. $\frac{5}{6} \times \frac{5}{7} = \frac{3}{28}$

G. $\frac{4}{5} \times \frac{2}{6} = \frac{7}{12}$
Q. $\frac{5}{7} \times \frac{2}{6} = \frac{7}{12}$

H. $\frac{1}{3} \times \frac{3}{9} = \frac{1}{9}$
R. $\frac{4}{5} \times \frac{3}{6} = \frac{4}{9}$

I. $\frac{3}{8} \times \frac{1}{6} = \frac{5}{8}$
S. $\frac{5}{8} \times \frac{1}{6} = \frac{1}{2}$

J. $\frac{3}{4} \times \frac{5}{9} = \frac{7}{15}$
T. $\frac{1}{2} \times \frac{2}{9} = \frac{1}{5}$

p. 100 — Five Across

A. $\frac{3}{8} \div \frac{2}{6} = 1\frac{7}{8}$ B. $\frac{3}{4} \div \frac{1}{2} = 1\frac{1}{2}$ C. $\frac{5}{13} \div \frac{5}{10} = \frac{2}{3}$ D. $\frac{1}{6} \div \frac{1}{12} = 2$

E. $\frac{4}{9} \div \frac{2}{3} = 1\frac{1}{3}$ F. $\frac{2}{9} \div \frac{1}{3} = \frac{1}{3}$ G. $\frac{6}{7} \div \frac{4}{12} = 1\frac{2}{7}$ H. $\frac{2}{3} \div \frac{1}{4} = \frac{2}{5}$

I. $\frac{9}{12} \div \frac{8}{10} = \frac{15}{16}$ J. $\frac{7}{8} \div \frac{2}{3} = 5\frac{1}{4}$ K. $\frac{5}{6} \div \frac{2}{7} = 2\frac{1}{3}$ L. $\frac{4}{9} \div \frac{2}{5} = 1\frac{1}{9}$

M. $\frac{2}{3} \div \frac{6}{9} = 1$ N. $\frac{5}{6} \div \frac{2}{9} = \frac{3}{5}$ O. $\frac{2}{3} \div \frac{2}{10} = \frac{5}{9}$ P. $\frac{3}{4} \div \frac{1}{12} = 3$

Q. $\frac{4}{9} \div \frac{6}{8} = \frac{8}{15}$ R. $\frac{4}{9} \div \frac{1}{3} = 2\frac{4}{7}$ S. $\frac{3}{4} \div \frac{4}{4} = \frac{1}{4}$ T. $\frac{1}{2} \div \frac{1}{5} = 4\frac{1}{3}$

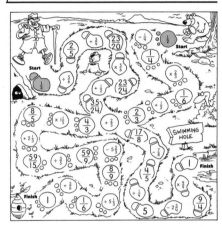

The winning card must have five answers crossed out in a row, column, or diagonal.

Which card won? **Card 1**

p. 101 — Fraction Hike

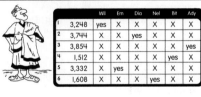

p. 102 — Ordering Fractions

Number sentences will vary.

p. 103 — Homework Machine

A. 1-7/8; 3; 6-2/3; 10; 3-3/4; 5-3/4
B. 1-1/4; 2-1/4; 1-2/3; 2-1/8; 1-15/16; 2-2/5
C. 5.703; 2.217; 34.69; 9.154; 721.09; 6.863
D. 318; 155; 526; 104; 28; 813
E. 8.58; 143.26; 64.74; 23.66; 43.68; 119.34

p. 104 — Number Logic

		Meg	Hio	Ian	Lea	Jil	Kar
A	64,520	X	X	X	yes	X	X
B	56,429	X	X	X	X	X	yes
C	117,571	X	X	X	X	yes	X
D	379,120	yes	X	X	X	X	X
E	80,417	X	yes	X	X	X	X
F	210,630	X	X	yes	X	X	X

1. Meg's number is **379,120** To the nearest ten thousand: **380,000**
2. Hio's number is **80,417** To the nearest ten thousand: **80,000**
3. Ian's number is **210,630** To the nearest ten thousand: **210,000**
4. Lea's number is **64,520** To the nearest ten thousand: **60,000**
5. Jil's number is **117,571** To the nearest ten thousand: **120,000**
6. Kar's number is **56,429** To the nearest ten thousand: **60,000**

Total: **908,687**   +   Total: **910,000**

p. 105 — Logic Blocks

1. 576 cubic units
2. 315 cubic units
3. 222 cubic units
4. 316 cubic units
5. 534 cubic units
6. 280 cubic units
7. 720 cubic units
8. 180 cubic units
9. 318 cubic units
10. Answers will vary.

p. 106 — Roman Logic

		Wil	Ern	Dia	Nel	Bit	Ady
1	3,248	yes	X	X	X	X	X
2	3,744	X	X	yes	X	X	X
3	3,854	X	X	X	X	X	yes
4	1,512	X	X	X	yes	X	X
5	3,332	X	yes	X	X	X	X
6	1,608	X	X	X	X	yes	X

Fill in the correct products.
A. Wil's product is **3,248**   B. Ern's product is **3,332**
C. Dia's product is **3,744**   D. Nel's product is **1,608**
E. Bit's product is **1,512**   F. Ady's product is **3,854**

p. 107 — What's Next?

1.

2. 1472, 2944, 5888, 11776

3. 7-sided figure, 8-sided figure, 9-sided figure

4. 6-digit number, 7-digit number, 8-digit number

5.

6. word that starts with "u," word that starts with "t," word that starts with "s"

7. (clocks)

8. three 5-letter words

9–10. Answers will vary.

p. 108 — Take It for a Spin

Answers will vary but must meet the criteria given.

p. 109 — Bat Magnets

1. will drop
2. should hang
3. should hang
4. should hang
5. may drop
6. should hang; may drop
7. may drop
8. should hang

p. 110 — Evergreens

1. 44 feet
2. 28 feet
3. 54 feet
4. 4 feet
5. 42 feet
6. 98 feet

Average Tree Height	
Tree	Height
blue spruce	44
Fraser fir	28
Norway spruce	54
red cedar	4
red pine	42
white pine	98

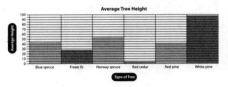

7. The trees were probably planted recently.
8. (30 + 60) ÷ 2 = 45; 45 − 4 = 41 feet
9. Cross out a and c.

p. 111 — Probability

Drawings may vary but must show the proper proportions.
1. 7/2; 7:2; 7 dimes for every 2 nickels
2. 9 to 2; 9/2; 9 bees for every 2 flowers
3. 1 to 1; 1:1; equal number of spoons and bowls
4. 4 to 1; 4/1; 4 nonfiction books for every 1 fiction book
5. 3/5; 3:5; 3 fractions for every 5 whole numbers
6. 1 to 5; 1/5; 1 red pencil for every 5 yellow pencils
7. 5 to 21 or 5:21
8. 17 to 21 or 17:21
9. 4 to 21 or 4:21
10. 1 to 5 or 1:5
11. 5 to 5 or 5:5
12. 0 to 5 or 0:5
13. 2 to 5 or 2:5
14. 0 to 5 or 0:5

p. 112 — Tree Diagrams

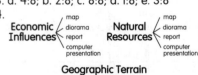

2. 8
3. a. 4:8; b. 2:8; c. 8:8; d. 1:8; e. 3:8
4.

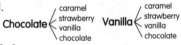

5. 12
6. a. 3:12; b. 4:12; c. 1:12

p. 113 — Class Assignment

1. No. There are only two other students assigned to that class.
2. Geometry. More students are assigned to geometry than algebra.
3. Orchestra. Most students are assigned to choir.
4. Chemistry A, geometry, swimming, and choir. These classes have the most students assigned to them.
5. 38:227
6. 60:105
7. 27:65
8. 227:385
9. 32:158
10. 35:385

Band Instruments Played			
Instrument	Fifth Graders	Sixth Graders	Total Number of Students
flute	27	38	65
clarinet	32	48	80
trumpet	45	60	105
percussion	14	21	35
other	40	60	100

p. 114 — Game Craze

1.

Day of the Week	Time	Time in Minutes
Sunday	2 hr. 15 min.	135
Monday	1 hr. 50 min.	110
Tuesday	1 hr. 45 min.	105
Wednesday	2 hr.	120
Thursday	1 hr. 50 min.	110
Friday	1 hr. 30 min.	90
Saturday	1 hr. 55 min.	115

2. a. 112; b. 110; c. 110
3.

White Knight
brown black white yellow
horse horse horse horse

Green Knight
brown black white yellow
horse horse horse horse

Black Knight
brown black white yellow
horse horse horse horse

Red Knight
brown black white yellow
horse horse horse horse

4. a. 4:16; b. 1:16; c. 8:16; d. 12:16

p. 115 — For the Birds

1. finch
2. red-winged blackbird
3. 82
4. 47 birds
5. 11 robins
6. red-winged blackbird, indigo bunting, oriole
7. She saw fewer than seven of these birds, so could not have seen one a day.
8. Answers will vary.

p. 116 — Raw Data

Graphs will vary but should represent the figures listed.
1. Mondo Coaster = 13, Whip-a-Round = 5, Gettin' Wet = 4, Free Fall = 5
2. China = 17, U.S.A. = 16, Japan = 5, Taiwan = 4, Korea = 1, Italy = 1, England = 3, Singapore = 1, Canada = 1, Malaysia = 1
3. (ranges may vary)
5:00–5:59 = 3, 6:00–6:59 = 4,
7:00–7:59 = 5, 8:00–8:59 = 4,
9:00–9:59 = 3, 10:00–10:59 = 2,
11:00–11:59 = 1, 12:00–12:59 = 1,
13:00–13:59 = 0, 14:00–14:59 = 1

pp. 118–119 — Amusement Park

1.

2. a. 30; b. 10; c. 5; d. 14.29 or 14
3. a. 5:100 or 1:20; b. 25:100 or 1:4
4.

5. a. 20; b. 15; c. 5, 15, 25; d. 14, 29
6. a. 25:100 or 1:4; b. 5:100 or 1:20
7.

8. a. 35; b. 10; c. 10 or 20; d. 14, 29
9. a. 35:100 or 7:20; b. 0:100
10. All are equally valid.
11.

Favorite Ride	Number of Visitors
Most Popular Roller Coaster	80
Round and Round	30
Wacky Wheel	30
Very Scary Coaster	75
Underwater Ride	25
Loopy Coaster	40
Up and Down	20

p. 120 — Gas Prices

1. a. 15¢; b. 13¢; c. 17¢; d. 13¢
2.

3. a. $1.46; b. $1.41; c. $1.37; d. $1.35; e. $1.34; f. $1.46; g. $1.48
4.

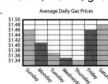

a. $22.20 − $20.10 = $2.10; $109.20
b. Thursday
c. Friday, Saturday, and Sunday
d. Wait to fill up until Wednesday or Thursday.